Becoming

Published by
BRIDGER HOUSE PUBLISHERS, INC
P.O. Box 2208, Carson City, NV 89702

1-800-729-4131

ISBN: 1-893157-07-5
13 digit: 978-1-893157-07-1

Cover design by The Right Type
Printed in the United States of America
10 9 8 7 6 5 4 3 2

Becoming

The question of "who?" is the focusing energy of the "messages" is a difficult question to answer tactfully and yet completely. "Isness" is the focus to be sought by each individual awareness. As each expands within the process of self-identification so does the ability to allow the flow of "Isness" to move through their experience. Each will attract into their awareness knowledge to live into wisdom. The vibratory rate of the planetary environment and of the members of humanity on Earth is low enough that this ability is currently virtually inaccessible. To assist willing members of mankind to access the necessary information to provide a way to transcend this current aberrant state, various volunteer awareness points within higher vibrational frequencies have acted as booster stations to focus this information through those willing to participate on the Earth plane. Knowing the custom of Earth's inhabitants requiring the "personify to identify" mode, names from the exotic to the ridiculous have been given as sources of this information. The information included exercises in discernment, most participants failed the discernment tests. Much was filled with profound truth, but much of it was drained of energy by the continual parade of victims wanting their personal problems solved for them. The information became distorted as the foci were withdrawn and the volunteers winged it (faked it) on their own for their sincerity was lost in the notoriety and greed that resulted.

In view of this history, it was the mutual agreement between the parties involved in the dictation/translation/transcription process for these messages that the foci involved would remain unidentified and there would be no monetary rewards whatsoever involved. Further, there would be no personal information disseminated for any one individual's benefit. The totality of the foci involved is for the benefit of the planet and its inhabitants, period! The truth of the messages is to be discerned and used for the benefit of humanity first and then gleaned by the individual to apply personally as part of the wholeness to which it is focused without the necessity of personal names to identify truth. If that is not understood, then the messages need to be read again to transcend this need into commitment to the holographic intention of the information they contain.

It is hoped that the succinctness of this message is accepted in the tone of importance in which it is intended. The window of opportunity to accomplish the necessary monumental consciousness transition is small compared to the obstacles within the human belief systems that must be literally dissolved so that the whole may be transformed.

It is sincerely hoped that the truth contained will be a sword that cuts through the armor of deception and lays open the hearts and minds of the necessary quotient for success.

Prologue

The messages contained in this, the third book of messages, are a continuation of information provided for the transition of the hearts and minds of those of humanity that are willing to be a catalyst for change. It is an undeniable truth that the current pattern of use and abuse of the planetary resources will lead to the end of its ability to sustain life forms. The human body and awareness are being deliberately overwhelmed physically, psychologically and magnetically. The majority of humanity fails to understand that unseen forces surrounding them are affecting their ability to survive. These are hidden within the "modern" conveniences powered by alternating electrical current; through radio, television, and many other low frequency emanations that now alter the individual's and the planet's magnetic fields to an unimaginable degree.

Just as human scientists experiment using what are considered "lesser species" with little concern for their suffering and death in the name of "scientific advancement," so also is humanity considered a lesser species to be used in like fashion. "You" are being used in exactly that way with the full knowledge and participation of those humans who believe themselves a part of the controlling hierarchy. These misguided humans are under the direct supervision of those beings that desire to continue to control this planet and others. The evolving conscious awareness of humanity has *again* evolved to a level that is considered dangerous. There are many that are now aware of this very real outside influence through the history revealed in the artifacts that were not destroyed or hidden, and by reaching logical conclusions about the sightings of various space craft as well as interaction with their occupants. These interactions have been both face to face and telepathic. The evidence indicates the presence of outside powers trying to continue the long standing control of Earth and its solar system. There are also those that are a positive presence hoping to be of assistance to an awakening humanity that must be willing to take on the responsibility for determining its own future in order to receive this available help.

Humanity has itself blocked the answer to its long standing cry for relief from enslavement by the outside forces, because it has been educated to ask for its "rescue" to come from an unknowable being that is in actuality a part of the controlling forces. Deception for control has been very successful for thousands of years. "Worship your controller" has been the ploy. Mankind has very little time left to wake up to this strategy and cooperatively agree that it is time to end this charade once and for all. Those who would assist must be a group that is willing to research and prove to itself beyond a shadow of a doubt the truth of this astounding pronouncement of the global situation. It must realize that humanity has to create its own future or remain in the circumstances of terrible slavery that are planned for them.

Both the positive and negative forces that are focused on this planet are aware that multiple cycles are culminating in this time sequence which will be to the advantage of either humanity or its colonizers, depending upon which one has the support of the overall planetary consciousness. This support can be either passively or actively understood. It can therefore be readily understood that if humanity does not make a clear choice to own this planet for itself, it is passively supporting continued enslavement and giving away its natural resources for the use of others rather than for itself. Rich mineral reserves have been transported from this planet and others in this solar system for thousands of years to enrich the lives of beings that have failed to steward their own planetary resources wisely. Reports of large "mother ships" are true and they are present for that purpose.

It is time for humanity to wake up and people to come together in the understanding that they are wise enough to control their own destiny and ask for help to "help themselves for the highest and best good for all concerned." That is a prayer that can be affirmatively answered! Until such time as humans can prove themselves to be cooperative and non-aggressive toward their benevolent neighbors, all help will be given indirectly: that is these beings will not walk among you until it is safe for them to do so. The help that can be offered will be very effective, but it must be asked for and accepted as assistance and not as rescue. A victim, be it individual or a planetary mass consciousness, has not evolved to a level of responsibility that warrants assistance. A victim consciousness must move through the need to look outside of itself and instead look at its own choices to find the cause(s) of its imperfect situation. Freewill is the freedom to choose, and all continuously choose, even if it is to choose not to choose. There are always forces willing to make choices for those unwilling to make their own. It is time for humanity to make its own choices. These messages were written to help with that important process.

III-1

The time of bringing the belief system into harmony with the actual physical reality situation in order to avoid the doom of destruction that is now awaiting the majority of earth's population is now. The important focus is not to dwell on the doom: it is the pivotal point that is now available to humanity that must be used as the impetus of change. Shocking as the facts are regarding the primrose path that humanity has been blindly following, these must be accepted and then the focus turned away from the deceptions toward creating a new reality.

What is this new reality? How can it be created if there is no knowledge of what it is that should or could replace the present situation? It would appear that this reality as it is created would be nothing but a hodge-podge of each one's desires based on the programming that is already present within each. Who would have the ability to release what is known and envision new concepts that would not be tainted with dreams of the past? If advice were asked of galactic brothers and sisters, would those not be entwined within their known reality? So it would appear that not only is there the surrounding current dilemma, but another one of even larger proportions insofar as breaking clear of the current one and then having to confront repetitions of experience rather than a new paradigm. This it seems is too much for a group consciousness that is or will be reeling from the shock of discovering the extent of their deception, or is it? It will be within the release of that shock and the decision to create their own reality that the birthing shall take place.

If what is known is deception, then will pursuing opposite concepts result in knowing truth? Indeed it could. For example, if benevolence has been sought from outside sources, is it indeed available from within one's own awareness? If freedom has not been found in either authoritarian systems or in the pursuit of individual freedoms, then where is it to be found? Could it be obtained within moral and ethical standards that gift the individual within an agreement made by co-operating groups? Could the size of the groups also be arranged by agreement? Could the groups find common ground for agreement within common desires for similar defined freedoms? If co-operation was the key ingredient rather than competition and the need to be/feel superior, then all things are possible. If common interest and desire were the defined beginning point around which all else is drawn by attraction to intended definition of desired experience, successful interaction is possible. If freedom to withdraw and find a more adequate experience within another group was encouraged and allowed, successful adventure in self-definition would be assured. The experience of the search for the most perfect expression could be an end unto itself. Though groups would be visited on a regular basis, it would be the commitment to a flexible and expanding focus that would enable them to continue until a satisfactory accomplishment was made by all involved. Thus no commitment to forever continuity would be a part of the goal, as expansive experience cannot place fences around itself and function within its intended expression. It is understood that expansive consciousness can only continue its expansion within a context of changing conceptual understandings. Progress results in shedding old understandings as these are encompassed in wisdom and the focus is ever toward the unfolding of new knowledge that allows for change. The introduction of apparently conflicting information resolves into integration of the apparent dichotomy and allows for progression into greater concepts. In other words, stagnation through holding to static beliefs halts the desired process. The safety of known apparent truths is a trap, which the progressing consciousness must purposefully avoid.

The ability to accept this conceptual understanding of the ground rules for participation within manifested experience requires a stretch in the belief system that is indeed quite phenomenal in and of itself. However mind boggling it is, it is the beginning point that is necessary if mankind is to extricate itself from the mire in which it now finds itself. The controlling over-lords are intent on returning this planet to a bare minimum of tightly enslaved beings so they can return to their original intent of stripping the needed minerals for the salvation of their own civilization at the expense of this planet and its inhabitants. It is the destiny of the inhabitants that belong to this planet by birth and adoption to take on the responsibility of changing this destiny and there is little sequential time remaining for them to accomplish this monumental feat. If challenge is the ingredient to call for the effort required, then certainly it is present. It is fervently requested that all those reading this material give it the most careful and focused consideration. It is further requested that each consider the call that is within it to assume the responsibility to make it happen, or to accept the results that acquiescence will reap without regret.

III-2

The days ahead do not look bright for those of you in the

USA. The dark plans appear to be coagulating into form as they have been planned. The light workers are the focus of "God," as you have chosen to name the outplay of creative energies that bring into being galaxies, solar systems, planets and individualized awareness to acknowledge and experience these manifestations. These now begin their work in earnest. Indeed each individual awareness has within itself that creative energy that is theirs to acknowledge and to know personally. It is the focus of that subtly powerful energy that is who each really is. It appears to be apart from the personality/ego that is capable of comprehending the understanding of the concept of it. *It is the "becoming" of this apparently larger than life beingness that is the difficult accomplishment.* Yet, there is "no other God." That which each is in this larger reality is the only doorway to understanding the concept of what is called God.

God is not a focus of personality – individual thought processes or a benevolent creator separate from you. God is the combination of the focus of all Its parts coalesced into the composite of all. Each awareness is blocked from being a part of that composite until each realizes that it is a part of this composite. Being told that it is, means nothing at all. It is the realization that one's self is a viable part of that composite that encompasses the totality of the being, that is what "becoming" is all about. One must become that reality and realize it is a viable aspect of the totality of God and that its input to that reality is the truth of who they are. It is not a mental realization, but one that registers total agreement within the mental, emotional, physical and spiritual levels of the total self. In other words, the spiritual aspect that focuses each into manifested reality finally gets the message through to the rest of its focus that is walking around in the body. The body must register this understanding through the totality of its brain-nervous system resulting in what is called a realization that then registers as a sudden feeling sensation accompanied by an all encompassing understanding. It allows for a total change in perception with regard to the self and how this self fits into the composite picture of experience. This results in a change in the perception of "God" which suddenly allows for an understanding that "God" equates to cosmic/galactic citizenship rather than a father/child relationship. It is a shift from "being or experiencing as powerless" to the awesome responsibility of being a contributing portion to the totality of what constitutes "God" or the creative energy of potentiality being focused into experience in order that it can be defined and understood.

The pivotal point at which this change takes place is not a shift from negative to positive. It is rather an uplifting to a new point in the spiral of experience that allows for a greater understanding and ability to utilize the positive/negative energies that are part and parcel of the outflow of creative energies in the individual and collective foci that result in the larger matrix or design of the whole pattern of a galaxy. It is easier to grasp the larger picture of this description than to define it at the level of each individual awareness. Each being comes to the point of their own realization in unique ways and by unique combinations of experience and wisdom. The point is often approached and rejected many times before the actual crossover acceptance happens. It requires a great deal of courage to crossover to a new and different perspective of the life experience. It requires releasing well-learned lessons and entering into a completely new consciousness of what reality truly is. For those who are on the planet Earth now, the deceptions are of such magnitude and the truth of what each being is, so well hidden, that the acceptance of the truth by the masses is such a gigantic leap in consciousness that it appears to be impossible that it could possibly happen. Yet, happen it must if this segment of the human race and this jewel of a planet are to survive.

When viewed from the larger perspective, the deceptions as perpetrated on the human race of this planet are so totally illogical that it is quite amazing that so few humans have figured out the truth. Granted, many when they are first introduced to the possibility that they have been deceived, immediately resonate with the idea and begin to contemplate its possibility and arrive at the truth of its probability. However, those that cling to the deceptions with tenacity are in the overwhelming majority. It is therefore to be anticipated that much chaos will be experienced before a mathematical coefficient of beings making the realization/change of consciousness is reached to bring about a shift in the future experience on this planet. It is then to be anticipated that the planet itself may or may not be able to survive the abuse that is being loosed upon it. To enable more help from the galactic citizenry to assist in this situation, a large number of "responsible Earth citizens" must request this help to save the planet first and the citizenry second. The requests now are being made more on a personal salvation basis than from the larger picture which automatically includes the personal aspect.

Thus it is that we offer these concepts for the consideration of those who choose to read and to accept them as suggestions worth considering and acting upon. Our concern is that the "composite concept of God" that each awareness is entitled to contribute to as a realized consciousness, become the next focus of concern for those awake and aware humans awaiting the next step in their assignment.

III-3

In the final accounting, it is the transition of consciousness into citizenship responsibility that is the goal. All else comes as a result of that choice. It was once offered as a part of the experience of bringing the US of A into being, but the consciousness of the individual people was not at a point that the goals could be maintained. Instead the exploiting of the resources through greed was greater than the commitment to soul agendas. Thus these experiences were allowed to be played out for the lessons to be learned. It is yet to be seen if these lessons will be discerned and brought into wisdom by a sufficient number to salvage this planet. Choices must be made to place the whole as equal to the individual in the consideration of the result desired.

Those asked to give their lives for the purposes of defending their country or placing the ideals of their leaders above those of others and attacking them, have allowed the illusion of a whole as being more important than the individual. It is a supreme sacrifice. When the whole and the individual consideration have equal weight, then war is not an option unless imbalance is acted out as an attack. Then all other options are considered first before a defense is appropriate. When there is balance, there is progress. It is to be remembered that the play of positive and negative energies brings forth the spiral of progress. However, the extremes of both bring forth regression, or loss of upward progress.

Another ingredient that must be taken into account within the context of war, is the familiar consideration of the victim consciousness. It is to be remembered that the law of attraction causes the victim to draw to its experience those who have a like consciousness but are on the other side of it, like the two sides of a coin. Those who feel abused draw to them those who will provide more of that experience until that attitude is shed. Thus war serves its purpose through forcing the victims to come together and experience the power of throwing off the aggressor. Then either the empowerment is retained, or the former victims return to one or the other side of the victim experience. This trading of sides continues until a realization is made that allows for transcending this experience. It is this outplay in the extreme that is upon this planet now.

It is understanding of this situation from its larger perspective that will allow those who are about assisting the planet and its inhabitants to move through these experiences and continue their chosen work. The experience for those involved cannot be changed for them. The consciousness within each involved group must shift and move both individually and collectively. The consciousness of the group that each leader represents will affect that leader's decisions. No amount of outside influence on that leader will change that and the only control that can be used is to "replace" that leader, usually through assassination. In that way the process can be slowed or changed by the chaos that accompanies the change in leadership, usually by tricking the group into believing the death of their leader was perpetrated by the other side. In this case, discernment is the key and it is the one time that the observer group may be able to influence the outcome by circulating the truth.

Through the comprehension of the larger picture, it is within possibility that those who have volunteered to assist the "God focus" can realize that their participation is a key to the transition of this planet and its inhabitants into a greater experience of manifested life. As taught by the religions at this time, personal power is transferred to and through an unknowable power and governmental bureaucracy. Both of these entities have been created for purposes of enslavement. The problem of education of the masses then presents itself. It is to be remembered, that it is the first few who are awakened and make the realization of this hoax that are the most difficult to convince of this reality. Thus, those precious few are to be valued and the education process continued for the process will become easier as the numbers increase. Though it seems but a pitiful few in view of the billions of beings that constitute the mass consciousness of the planet, it must be remembered that it took the opposition literally eons of time to reach the current control level.

A change in the understandings that they have slowly and carefully nurtured can be accomplished in a very, very short time because they defy logic. The mind of conscious beings constantly searches for logic in order that each may stay positioned within the linear perception of time and life experience. Illogic is a form of chaos and to assimilate illogic into a logical sequence requires a great deal of concentration. It is one of the reasons that rest or recreation away from this process is craved. Once illogical ideas are identified, then the sequential thought process reprograms itself, rather like a computer changing its internal arrangement of data to a more efficient combination of sequences. When illogic is perceived and the rearrangement of data takes place, then other illogical data is identified and the search is on to further identify any other illogical data present and to eliminate it also. Through this process, great changes in the mass consciousness can be accomplished.

III-4

As the Light Workers on this planet comprehend the larger picture, it is helpful to them to continue to broaden the picture to include a greater understanding of the galactic wholeness in which they are playing such an important part. This understanding is to enable them to enhance their observer roles and thus see through and past the chaos that each will find going on around them. Through the process of observation while experiencing the chaos, each will be able to place themselves in a position that allows them to be in places of safety, not in hiding, but in movement within the chaos. It is an experience of observing the self in movement, a process of literally being in two fields of awareness simultaneously. Simply put, an example to begin the process is being aware that each individual is at the same moment in sequential time an individual with its own life agenda and also a part of the family, community, state, nation and planetary whole. Each status is an awareness that is separate and yet a composite of the whole earthly experience. Each shifts their thought processes between each role and yet maintains their stability.

Further, a truly good actor can be their own personality and can also assume the personality of the character they are playing and move between them without losing the awareness that they are both. The Light Workers, ground crew, whatever each chooses to call him/herself, must learn to walk in two worlds simultaneously. It would be wise for each to begin to practice the art of this split awareness. It is nothing more than an acceptance of the situation as it is. There is the world of deception and the world of knowing that the deception is being perpetrated on the planetary inhabitants.

Each also knows that a new and different world of experience awaits birthing, but until the one that is known to the inhabitants begins to crumble into chaos, there is no way to birth the new one. As the current known reality reaches a specific degree of disintegration in the chaos, the new one can begin to come into manifested reality. The question is which one will materialize, the one planned by the dark planners or the one that is envisioned by the Light Workers/Ground Crew and those drawn to the dream of the New Paradigm. There is the planned world of disharmony with the galactic composite plan or one that is created in harmony with it. The critical number of humans desiring a harmonious existence within the surrounding energies of potentiality that constitute this Galaxy must be reached in order for the New Paradigm to come into a reality recognizable by those beings in harmony with it. Based on a mathematical formula it is less than might be thought considering the number of humans on Earth. One of the reasons for this is that those who desire this harmonious experience will be focused upon that desire. Even though there are many humans that are now focused on the deception, during the

Becoming

chaos they will lose that focus and become caught up in the chaos. Their focus will be on the chaos, thus nullifying a great deal of the power that those of dark intent have established. It is during this time that the most important work for the Light (those of positive intent) will be done. This is the reason that it is important for those of positive focus to become aware of their purpose for being here and learn to lift themselves out of the influence of the chaos and know that those will be the moments of most productive service to this planet and thereby to their fellow humans. The exact knowledge of the nature of the New Paradigm is not all that important at this time, it is the desire **for it** that is important. It is the commitment to being part of the positive/Light focus that is important. It is the practice of walking within more than one awareness by acknowledging them as a part of everyday living that is primary. Each must learn to choose in the moment which awareness is the predominant one and change from one to the other by intent.

Awareness is the focus of who and what each is. Each has a multifaceted opportunity to learn to use latent/unused abilities that are available. The knowledge and use of these have been hidden and denied, for to use these would bring freedom from control. There are many that would seem quite miraculous. These are indeed simple applications of mathematical laws that exist but are unknown. Many of these will be included in the lessons to follow, not explained in confusing terminology, but as guided, simple lessons in application. When practiced and applied to daily living situations, they will become a part of each one's life experience and available when needed in the experiences coming in the sequential times to come.

It is suggested that each begin to observe the various roles that are available in situations and thoughts about situations in daily experience such as being part of the deception and observing the deception. During one's thoughts, which role is being played out, the family member, the citizen of the local community, the church member, the dismayed U.S. citizen when learning of the latest aggression by the government, the state citizen reading the news of the latest activity in the legislature, etc., etc. What observer role or active role is each one (are you) playing in the moment? Is it the role that you desire to play? If not, then can you change "hats" so to speak and observe from a different role? It is important that each of you learn to discern through self observation where you are in the scenario that is occurring in your perception at any given moment. In the practice of this role playing, much safety in the future can be gained.

III-5

In the days to come, those who intend to hold the focus for this transition of the planet and its inhabitants will need every positive word to encourage them to continue in the process. It is the intent of this material to add to the positive intent of those committed to the project by providing practical and easily used techniques to assist in holding this intent in place. It is necessary that this intent be held on a continual basis by the constant input of many. Inasmuch as manifestation can be traced backward to thought, to light, to intent/focus, to potentiality, it can be seen just where the intent to participate in this process fits into the flow of creation. For whatever purpose, be it positive or negative, the process is the same and available to be used. It is the ease of the flow, that makes the difference, for as the previous material has revealed, when the intent/focus resonates with the higher creational intent manifestation results more easily. Any desired manifestation that is in harmony with the higher/finer intent receives reinforcing energy and therefore is able to receive advantageous assistance in manifesting without needing to be aware of what it is or how it came. In other words, that which resonates with the greater plan of wholeness draws to it through the law of attraction added supportive energy.

Manifestation that lacks this resonance and is initiated at a level below the highest source of purpose or intention requires a more intense focus and careful attention to the continual need to hold the plan firmly in the center of attention. The smallest detail that deviates from the plan can cause a ripple effect that changes the planned outcome at many levels of the manifestation process. There is no automatic support process to dovetail these changes into the plan harmoniously. This then makes the resistive plan vulnerable to deviations that can be devastating to the total plan without the knowledge of those initiating it and holding it in place with their intention.

It is important that those who are supporting the manifestation of the New Paradigm understand this and hold this comparison of the difference of the two sets of circumstances that underlay the situation at hand that they have chosen to participate within firmly in mind. It is entirely possible that by being familiar with as many of the details of the opposition's plans, discouraging and demoralizing as they appear to be, when deviations do occur in it, it is possible to sense the panic and frantic activity that goes on as attempts are made to counteract the effects the deviation may have wrought. Those are then occupied in making changes in the details of the overall plan to compensate for the effects that naturally ripple through the entire situation. This then opens the possibility of being able to add to the effects to further complicate the recovery they are trying to accomplish.

Thus we offer two tools for holding the focus for the New Paradigm firmly in place. The first being the understanding of the overriding higher purpose of the creational flow bringing with it intelligent coordination of energies that resonate with the higher purpose. The second using the greatest possible understanding of their plan as the basis of observing their process and finding moments and opportunities to add to their complications in maintaining their focus. Simply focusing attention on their dilemmas can place great stress on their ability to correct the flow of intentional energy, for that which is contrary to the Light, must be done in secrecy and darkness. Knowledge is thought which flows from the Light of understanding. This then points out the need to know as much as possible about the plans of the dark intention for the enslavement of this planet. It points out the importance of the work that has been done by those committed to investigating, observing, drawing obvious conclusions and then sharing with any and all who will listen and read about what constitutes the dark plans. Those who have committed their life focus to exposing this plan serve their fellow human beings and this planet well. This information is critical to the transition through this process that must be made by the planet and its inhabitants. It must not be the focus, but must be the background upon which the New Paradigm will begin its building process out of the chaos that the dark plan will cause. Thus in its own way, looking at the bigger picture, the situation instigated by the dark forces will in the long run serve that portion of humanity and the planet that choose to take advantage of the opportunity offered as a boost on their path of evolvement.

III-6

The rapidity of the coming events into manifestation has been allowed in that the chaos will serve the birth of change. Though those of you who dread its onset, knowing the additional suffering that will be endured by the many you consider the pawns of innocence is understood, yet indeed are they innocent? The same opportunities that have been afforded you, though they may have been clothed in different appearances, have been offered to all. It is the few that have opened their conscious thought to the possibilities and the probabilities that now find themselves in awareness of what the true picture is that faces the planet and its inhabitants. This group must also understand that the dilemma will be solved in what is called Divine Order. This process moves in a holographic, nonlinear process that accomplishes its purpose within chaos much more rapidly than within what is perceived as order. What appears as order now is indeed the rigid confines of institutions of experience that are out of balance within the galactic matrix of progress toward expansive progress or evolvement.

Those who serve the focus of intention to bring this planet back into the flow of progress within the overall matrix must bring the center of their attention to this intent.

At the moment, it is possible to visualize this planet as poised within a back flow or eddy that is out of the movement of this ever-present flow. Only through the focused intent of this special group can it be drawn back to its position within that flow. Visualization in unison or agreement is the most powerful tool available. It is through the *Handbook of the New Paradigm, Embracing the Rainbow* and this book to the known few who are at this time actively focusing their thought energy to this purpose, that this agreement in active corrective movement can be made known. Though the group doing this seems pitifully small, it is extremely effective. Those involved in this activity are not entities of small experience or ability. This is not the first time any of these has served the forces that organize in times of imbalance that brings opportunity for leaps forward in expression and expansion for this or other galaxies. This is not meant to feed the ego, but that each may begin to recognize that there is great power within their commitments. The time willingly spent in individual and collective focus on the desire and intent to literally focus this planet through this difficult process of evolvement is well worth the effort involved. As this focus is made within a continuing commitment, the law of attraction will draw to it the sufficient number to begin the momentum of energies that will bring about the movement within the mass consciousness necessary to refocus the alignments that currently exist. It is through the recognition and acceptance of the possibility by each of those who read these named books and circulated materials that this focus will build upon itself within a mathematical format that will underlay the process.

It is necessary that each lay aside modesty and reluctance

to accept the possibility that each is indeed a special and powerful entity that has donned a robe of obscurity and forgotten their origins that each might remain unknown not only to yourselves, but to those of evil intent until this present moment. It is time to assume the proper identity and come into the role of service as was agreed upon before this series of lifetimes was accepted as part of the service contract. It is time to realize that this is who and what you are and what you do and have done before. It is a matter of simply remembering and adapting what you innately know to fit the current requirements. A certain amount of reluctance is natural because of the human format that contains your awareness. It is understood that this involves a literal containment, or restriction upon your ability to realize your true identity. Thus these messages continue the process of awakening your remembrance, stimulating your desire to participate and applying pressure to your commitment to this project.

As you contemplate the possible truth of these words, within your inner awareness the energies contained in this process do their work and the truth begins to root itself and grow. That which constitutes your segment of the "mission impossible," as it seems to the conscious mind, begins to be drawn into your daily experience. A knowingness of what is appropriate and necessary is apparent and seems the only possible thing to do. It will not seem that what you do as a part of your daily experience will be at all heroic, but through the combination of these daily contributions by the growing group committed to this project, much will be accomplished. It is in the accomplishment of these seemingly small contributions that the rooted truth of who and what you are will grow. At the moment of necessity when each must stand forth within that identity and declare the truth of the future of this planet, the ability to do so will bring a natural, powerful and pivotal shift that will cause the desired transition to occur. It is knowing that the needed commitment to the totality of the necessary change does not require great personal sacrifice or the need to stand alone before the forces of evil and suffer great bodily harm that allows for the commitment to service to be accepted with enthusiasm.

Though we admit there are a few exceptions to this pattern of service, those who accept these roles are well aware of their identities and their commitment to this level of service. To these few, loyalty, special help and guidance is constantly at hand. Blessed indeed are these special beings of commitment to leadership within this focus of service.

III-7

The human forms that reside on this planet have long been held in bondage and kept from the natural evolvement that enables each to enter into the true understanding of their source and purpose for experiencing manifested existence. The knowledge of the laws that govern this galaxy has been withheld and purposeful teaching has been denied. Instead deception has been the basis of all knowledge given. It is the decision of the overseers of this galaxy to end this practice here and now. However it must be the individual and collective choice of the inhabitants of this planet to change this experience. The long-standing deceptions have rooted and grown within the understandings of the human consciousness. Thus the decision by the Galactic Counsel will have little or no effect until the residents of this planet choose to change their experience. However, the ability to make the change once accepted and decided upon by earth's human residents will flow easily and irrevocably once the sufficient percentage of those desiring change has been reached.

What exactly the Galactic Council will decide to do to assist this is now the question. It means that those who are misusing the laws that underlay manifested existence no longer have the same degree of energy input to support their activities as they have had at their disposal. There will be a waning or lessening of this supportive energy. This will bring about an unraveling of their overall plan. Those carefully planned strategies will begin to have unexpected results that will cause unexpected ripple effects that do not bring about either the expected results or the degree of expected results in order to accomplish the anticipated goal.

The plan as known to those awake and aware humans is "the plan." It is their anticipated and embroidered plan. It is not necessarily what that plan is in reality. It is important that the difference be understood clearly. The actuality of "the plan" is skeletal indeed. It is open to many variations and has many weaknesses that are unknown to them. It is in the best interest of those who desire a change in the opportunities and experiences that are available to the beleaguered members of humanity to know that their intentions to change the momentum and outcome of this carefully laid plan of enslavement are the arrows of destruction to that plan. It is the intention to withdraw support of, belief in and participation within "the plan" that will cause it to collapse of its own weight. Within the outflow of creative expansive energies, the directional flow is based on intentional purpose.

The plan of enslavement is based on the intention to destroy and enslave large portions of humanity as a method of solving a problem that was caused by those who have controlled this planet and its inhabitants. This situation was brought about by the controllers' own decisions regarding the use of the planet and its inhabitants in the very beginning. This has been further complicated by the addition of various groups of humanity from various other places in the galaxy being added to the citizenry against their will. There does then exist a complex citizenry that brings to the mix an interesting dilemma for those who desire to control the planet.

There is a direct opposition of intentions, those of slavery and those of freedom. If it were not for the added citizenry, the plan of enslavement would have been accomplished long ago. Those that were in the beginning literally engineered for the purpose of serving were left devoid of many human characteristics for that intentional purpose of enslavement. However, the genetic addition of the added citizenry has now spread throughout the planetary bloodlines. Though there are still pockets of pure genetic variations within the whole, there exist a large percentage of genetic combinations that confuse the understandings of those who plan to control the citizens. Unexpected actions and reactions continue to upset the carefully laid plans.

It is, therefore, important that those who intend for this situation to play out differently than the planned scenario understand that their intention to create a different ending to the current flow of events has the ability to accomplish this. Once this understanding is accepted, the commitment to it becomes easier and more realistic to the conscious awareness. It is much like the laser sword of your popular movie. That intention, which is in harmony with the galactic intention for evolvement through freewill choice of experience, then becomes a powerful tool of change in the "hands" of those who understand its usefulness and learn to wield it in a timely fashion and at moments of greatest effect. Through the knowledge and understanding of the intentions of the opposing force, this understanding can be used to great effect for the purpose of freeing this planet from its heretofore use as a source of minerals and as a dumping grounds for human misfits. It is through the realignment of genetic combinations that evolvement to more complex levels has occurred for a percentage of inhabitants. This percentage now brings forward the necessary quotient to allow for the transition of this planet into Galactic citizenship, when these can be awakened and bound together by intention to take advantage of this opportunity.

III-8

As the willing members of those in human focus awaken to the plight that surrounds them, it is clear to them that the situation is indeed serious and that no amount of physical resistance can change this. It is apparent that something else must be done to bring a change to their future experience on this planet. Through the consideration of the larger picture, it also becomes clear that the lack of understanding of not only the history of their origins, but the lack of a true purpose for existence on this planet has left them bereft and adrift like flotsam on the sea. At the basis of each one's awareness there is a weary wonderment that says to each, "why bother." "What reason is there that is worth striving for to maintain life in this physical body?" "Where is this Utopia that is promised as a reward for the effort that must be put forth in this human experience?" "Does it even exist?" "Is there only a short rest before we begin over again with another life of disappointment and frustration?" "Why is there such a sense of participating in a spiral of experience that leads to the 'same ole, same ole,' or even less, each lifetime?"

There is a song that says the answer is "blowing in the wind!" The wind of change! There is a point at which the thought patterns mentioned above reach a place within the consciousness that causes a shift. A purpose is sought, not in the world of the 5 senses that is called reality, but within the awareness. Each, within every lifetime, is called upon to find their purpose, not in the world of effort, but from within the space of awareness that is only found at the center of the "awareness that knows itself." This awareness of the self was the **gift** from the "tree of knowledge" that the religious soothsayers have spent so much time attempting to teach as a great mistake. This is the gift that lifted humanity out of the animal kingdom and placed them at the edge of the kingdom of those beings that "know who and what they are." So who and what are they? Beings that are little, if any different than what you who is reading this is. They may have greater use of their brain capacity that enables them to know and do things that seem miraculous to those of lesser understanding. However, if you look at the progress made in that area in the past century on this planet, that is of little consequence in the dilemma of knowing who and what you are in the search for this greater acquisition of knowledge. Are these "gods" that have come and gone from this planet at their will and left you in such awe of their accomplishments that you worship them as all knowing, really all knowing?

Through the research of the artifacts of past civilizations that are now available and have been studied, cataloged and conclusions drawn, it is clear to the few that have availed themselves of this knowledge, that humanity has been lead down the primrose path. One ideology after another has been thrust upon innocent mankind in their search for their purpose and their origins to keep them in darkness and ignorance. The question is why? What purpose could beings of more intelligence have for deliberately causing their planetary relatives to be misled and their evolutionary progress diverted into a backwater rather than leading them onward and upward into full citizenship and responsibility within the Galactic family? Could there be a character flaw within the genetic expression of that particular group of beings? Could that character flaw have been carried on through to those of humanity that have the intermingled blood of those particular apparently superior beings?

The expansive flow of the Universal energies that underlay the manifestation of potentiality into expression requires that knowledge be experienced into wisdom. There is at the center of all, infinite patience for this to be accomplished within non-linear expression. This is a concept that the human mind, unless fully activated, has great difficulty in understanding. Within holographic experience, simultaneous interactions are occurrings without the limitations of linear, sequential time frames. In other words, what appear to those of less active mind/brain capabilities as experiences happening one after the other are indeed being played out in other experiential formats simultaneously. Thus a picture is being completed with more than one activity going on with no time constraints for beginning or completion, for all is in constant motion with only momentary rest periods of inactivity. These momentary periods of inactivity are those incidents of realization of wisdom acquired through the experiencing of knowledge to points of understanding. Thus wisdom is gained so that the process is continued expansively.

The apparent character flaws that have held mankind in a delusional state of false and misleading knowledge that is impossible to experience into wisdom, has been a two fold situation. First the flaw by the more knowledgeable, self appointed over-lords of this planet who have jealously guarded their perceived superiority and the flaw of humanity in thinking they are lessor and thus the pawns of these beings. Because ones have less understanding does not make them of less potentiality. It is potentiality that is the measure of worth and mankind has equal potentiality with any and every other expression of self awareness. It is in making this realization and demanding the opportunity to self-express into this potentiality that will free mankind on this planet to accomplish this purpose. This demand as a personal decision made within each one's own inner knowingness will bring about the change from victim/slave to sovereign owner of his/her future individually and collectively. It is a rising up from within that will in proper order progress into the reality of known experience for this planet. How long this process will take within the linear time reality that is processed through the human ego (the ability to observe) at this stage of evolution remains to be chosen by humanity itself.

III-9

The record of advancement insofar as humanity on this planet is concerned, is a checkerboard of dark and light, or positive and negative experience. As an overall composite from the point of view of a spiral of upliftment, the results are dismal to say the least. Whatever help has been given has been convoluted and shamefully diverted into disinformation. What has been intuited has been hidden or destroyed and those gifted humans imprisoned or killed. Mankind has been purposefully held in mental, emotional and spiritual captivity. The age-old question arises as to "why God allows this to happen?" Here again we face the fallacy of what "God" has been represented to be. The question is addressed to an outside Supreme Being that holds power over each individual life expression. It is the transfer of the awe held long ago when beings of apparent superior status brought forth the human in partial likeness of themselves for the purpose of exploiting their physical forms in slavery to an all knowing superior being that promises benevolence but seldom provides it. In other words, this "God" with the expected power to control all things, does not now and never has existed.

It is the self-awareness attribute that is within each individual that is available to each and every being that has risen above animal status that is available to be harnessed and directed and will provide the benevolence "each feels it deserves." Here we face the attribute that allows for exploitation by outside influence. This brings the focus back to the understanding that each has of who and what they are. The self-awareness of each has the ability to choose and decide how to experience their manifested reality. It is the power that either takes them forward into greater experience through wisdom gained or allows them to regress into lesser experiences of slavery and degradation. These are made, not in one great decision, but as a sum total of all the experiences from early childhood onward. Unfortunately, these decisions are greatly influenced by the parent's experience from conception forward. Thus we find each generation saddled with the difficulty of overcoming this influence plus the planned misconceptions that are planted by those pawns of the self appointed overlords of this planet.

Only through recognizing and accepting this dilemma in its true dimensions can those committed members of this human race find a place of equilibrium from which to begin to build a viable understanding of who and what they are. It is necessary to accept that the totality of human status is yet to be attained. It is totally possible to attain the full active status of the human potentiality, but it indeed will require assistance. This assistance, as has been stated before in these lessons, can be made available after a sufficient number of humans on this planet accept the fact that their help must first come from within their own decision process. It is a prerequisite that there must be acceptance that their only rescue is to be found in their own inner resources. Only after this realization may they ask for help from their galactic brothers and sisters. The "God" so sought by the disillusioned members of humanity as a source of rescue exists only as the composite of all manifested awareness as focused within the confines of each expanding unit of awareness ad-infinitum. It is necessary to recognize and decide to become a part of this manifested awareness as a responsible and contributing part of it in order to proceed within its process.

At this point, the question of the misuse of humanity by its self-appointed overlords returns to the focus of this discussion. As brought forth within the prior discussion, the laws that allow for potentiality to express into manifested reality so that knowledge can be experienced into wisdom and progress provide the basis for this process. The basic law, is the law of attraction. Thus, mankind on planet earth has been influenced from the beginning to maintain the understanding that knowledge and wisdom come from those of greater and superior knowledge and wisdom. Further that this knowledge and wisdom is given out to them through adoration and worship of those holding this superior understanding. This has brought an understanding that the humans on this planet exist at the whim of those holding this superior wisdom. As time has passed, this understanding has been manipulated into the belief by humanity that it is vested in an unknowable awareness that has all the attributes as wielded over them by their overlords. These ever present beings have hidden themselves and operated through this "unknowable God," holding humanity hostage not only for the resources of the planet, but as a last experiment in manipulation and literal entertainment. It has previously been referred to as their own "virtual reality computer game." Unfortunately that is more truth than fiction.

The collected or mass consciousness of the humans on this planet in accepting this situation as depicted has resulted in the attraction of those who are willing to exploit this total belief system. This is within the action of the Universal Laws. It will remain so until humanity literally pulls itself out of this situation. It is the desire of those of your galactic brothers and sisters who are aware of your planetary dilemma that you come into the realization of what is the true situation. There is not an easy way to accomplish this inasmuch as the human belief systems are so deeply ingrained with false information and deceptions. The hope is that the frustrations of enough of humanity have reached a great enough degree for them to begin to accept the possibility that virtually everything they have been taught to understand is inaccurate. The most important new understanding to be accepted is that without personal responsibility to change each person's consciousness with regard to understanding who and what each one is, this situation will not change. The whole of the planetary belief system will change only as its individual members change until a critical mathematical quotient is reached. How long this takes will depend on the spread of this understanding throughout all the groups that are now on this planet. It is the responsibility of those who come into the understanding of this information to disseminate it. Then and only then will the future change.

III-10

As the plan for control of this planet calls for the shutting down of the freedom of even the thoughts of the inhabitants, so also at the same time the desire to expand their experience becomes activated. It is the inability to connect with the greater aspect of each that allows the controllers to continue the closing down of the human awareness. The controllers believe that they are solely responsible for the creation of the human beings that inhabit this earth. Through genetic manipulations made in laboratory experiments and by birthing the first chemically manipulated embryos through their own bodies, the controllers believe the resulting humans are their product and solely their possessions. What they do not recognize is what might be called the Divine connection that was present in the first place. The basic being that was available in the beginning was not of their creation and thus contained the possibility of evolving into fully functioning humans within their own time line. Those were present on this planet through the focus that indeed holds even the controllers within their own expression.

It is necessary to go back further in the process of the laws of the Universe allowing for manifested awareness to be present. Potentiality has birthed itself to explore the possibilities that are inherent within it. In order to do this; there must be the ability to observe its processes of doing this. The ability to observe is what is called awareness. Thus to create situations, circumstances and observable phenomena and explore the results, there must also be present within the totality the ability to observe and draw conclusions with regard to this process. The result is that various foci of this ability to observe, experience and draw logical conclusions have created endless varieties of foci with various abilities to do this. Each and all do this in their own way and the sum total of their experience influences the potentiality of expression within a given greater focus. In this way, by expanding the consciousness in an attempt to gain a view of the greater picture, it can be concluded that the positive/negative experiences feed their data into the greater awareness of this collective focus.

Through a lack of understanding of the overall purpose of self-awareness and the presence of this greater awareness, these individual centers become caught up in their own experience, thus cutting themselves off from the totality to which they belong. What might be called power trips happen. There is within your vernacular a cruder saying that refers to this situation. So, in this moment, humanity is sitting in the middle of that reference. Because of one ingredient within the format of the Universal laws, the responsibility for curing this type of situation must remain with those experiencing it. This ingredient is called freewill, or choice, or the responsibility of decision. Humanity has the freewill to choose to change its experience or to continue the current experience. This is not a new thought within the continuity of these messages, that is because there is no other solution. Because of this, it is repeated over and over from as many contexts and approaches as can be presented in order to make this point as clear and as emphatic as possible.

Needless to say, if there were another way, it certainly would have been brought forth in the information that is being made available to you. It is imperative that the responsibility for creating this change in experience be firmly planted within the attitude and understanding of as many human minds as possible. The possibility of being able to do this seems remote in the context of the overwhelming control measures that are being thrust upon you. That in itself should indicate that such measures are necessary in order to overwhelm the powerful potentiality that the human mind, once organized into a common opinion or focus, has within it. When mankind does direct its focus within the understanding of its power to create through agreement to hold a single focus, there is no way in which it can be overwhelmed, particularly if that focus is in harmony and agreement with other citizens within the surrounding galactic community.

The question then arises as to how to bring a squabbling group of opinionated beings into agreement. The controllers are attempting to do this, only for the purposes of its focus. In regimenting the thoughts of humanity toward their goal they are also regimenting the sub-conscious thought patterns more and more toward resistance and opposition to their planned goals. In other words, they are also helping to set up the possibility of the failure of their plans. In past experience, their plans have worked to keep humanity under their control. This time, however, their human counterparts are more intelligent, far more educated and have tasted more freedom than ever before. This gives them a greater opportunity to come together in agreement, particularly with the yet present ability to connect via the communication capabilities available. Though plans to bring this capability to an end are definitely formulated, there is yet opportunity to access them to great advantage.

It is hoped that these messages, though containing shocking and discouraging content, also offer hope and suggest opportunities that can be put to use by those of mankind that are awake and aware. The future may yet hold promise for the transition of the planet and it inhabitants into true freedom to return to the path of evolvement. The future need not be dark with the promise of continued slavery.

III-11

As each reader moves through the various stages of encompassing the reality of the greater picture of humanity and its plight of the moment, the process of accepting changing perceptions becomes a familiar experience. The material has thus far begun at a simple level and progressed through levels of understanding. We are now at a place to begin encompassing the understanding of those that would continue holding humanity in captivity. Just as they have attempted to know humanity's capabilities for **their** purposes, it is also necessary that **they** be understood. Though their understanding of humanity has failed to include the "divine" connection which they have claimed exclusively as their own, humanity's other attributes are well understood. In order for those that have contemplated the information within these messages to have a clear and balanced understanding of the entire picture, it is important to know more about their counterparts.

The expansive flow of creation extends itself not only in the manifestation of more planets, stars, galaxies, etc., it also allows for limitless expansion of the awareness. It is difficult for the mind/brain that is not operating at its full capacity to contemplate the concept of what limitless and timeless could mean. Within this concept there is allowance for forays into both positive and negative expression that feed back to the wholeness of knowledge and wisdom within a collective composite. In the consideration of the wholeness, then each individual awareness seems like a grain of sand on the beach and causes each to then wonder as to the importance of their personal experience. Is it of such little value that pain and suffering are meaningless to this composite awareness? Is it even aware of all of its parts? Here again the mind/brain that has been focused only upon itself and its personal experience has cut itself off from this wholeness of which it is a part. It is the contemplation of the wholeness and its meaning that allows for participation within it. It is in stretching the awareness to purposefully include itself within the composite that its importance to that composite becomes known.

Having come forth through the auspices of a group awareness that is focused upon its own importance, that attribute has carried through to humanity. In contemplating a new paradigm of experience, it is this key of including itself within the composite wholeness rather than focusing only upon itself that will bring forth the freedom that humanity has as the impetus for change. To put this in less abstract terms, it is the desire to become participating members of the galactic family and to extend their perception that the purpose of life experience is greater than each individual experience and each planetary experience that will bring this forth. When it is realized that harmony of experience is found by expressing within the immutable Laws of the Universe and not in ignoring them, then experience can be shaped into progress and joyful expression. Recognizing these laws as the basis within which all manifestation is expressed, it becomes possible to recognize imbalance for what it is and to transcend it.

Technological progress is not a true measure for progress within the creative expansion of potentiality. Those who have focused primarily on this one purpose often destroy their creation through misuse of that focus. It has sometimes caused the distortion of the progress of others, a situation with which humanity on this planet can certainly identify. In this way, those who are again attempting to play at their control and destruction games have placed this planet and its inhabitants in danger of destruction.

Imbalance as projected through failure to recognize the potentiality of self-aware beings to pursue their inherent evolvement processes has brought both the givers and the receivers of this policy to a point where the significant decisions each will make will influence their progress. Each will reap the results of these decisions. Each has the potential power to change the path of their evolvement by the actions taken through the next few sequential events to be shaped by the decisions made both individually and collectively.

It is important to grasp that the individual does influence the collective decision, both directly and indirectly. What that means is that though the individual is bound by the group decision through composite agreement, it also allows for that individual to free itself from the group decision by forming or becoming a part of a smaller group with a different focused purpose. This smaller focused group, by invoking the second Law of the Universe, the focus of intentional manifestation, then separates itself from the greater group and does change the path or experience of its evolvement. It is for this reason that the messages have encouraged the formation of smaller groups with the intended purpose of creating a New Paradigm of experience. Those who have evolved beyond the need to participate in the victim consciousness that holds them within the grasp of the controlling civilization and locks the two groups into this situation as it now exists, have the opportunity to salvage this planet and its inhabitants. They may at least create an opportunity for a sizeable group to free itself from this situation. It must be stressed that a quorum must be met in order for this to occur.

It is suggested that this information be contemplated with serious consideration for the opportunity that is within it.

III-12

What is a major drama to the inhabitants of earth is indeed an important pivotal point in the continuing evolution of conscious manifested awareness. In the totality of the galactic expression that constitutes the known reality, it is wondered how this small, beautiful planet at the outer reaches of this defined area can carry such importance. It is the transition through the taking back of personal power/control of individual and collective destiny that is the central issue. Just as the consciousness of the leader of a country, self-appointed or elected, expresses the composite consciousness of the people within that country, the planetary scenario that is being played out is the collective representation of the consciousness of the beings on that planet. This then is carried out into a further composite of consciousness in an expanding composite. We might say that earth is the collection point of victim consciousness, a point within a larger collective of this unhappy experience within this area of the galaxy. The solving of this situation by humanity on this planet will bring forth a clearing of this experience in an expansive ripple effect that will reach to the far corners of the galaxy. When visualized in a holographic context, it is indeed a "big deal."

Because of the freewill aspect of Universal Law, it becomes clear that the burden of accomplishment that is carried by mankind at this moment is one of great importance. While it is understood by the counterparts who intend to hold humanity as their own to do with as they please, there is much interest in their attitude and treatment of those on this planet. There is no apparent intention to redirect this continuing pattern of enslavement. This presents the dilemma of how to assist humanity and answer their calls for freedom from this experience. It also accounts for the concentrated effort on the part of the self appointed colonizers of this planet to maintain claimed ownership through members of the human race that are willing to be pawns. In this way, it may be portrayed that the control is not from outside, but indeed by humanity enslaving itself. As the saying goes, "saying something is true, does not make it true!"

Because the belief patterns of humanity, through governments, religions, education and media have apparently so successfully shut down the minds of the greater portion of the people, it is the opinion of the controllers that the game is won. Even though they are quite sure of this, they yet are careful to keep all aspects in careful review. However, within the group of pawns there are factions of competition for the favor of the controllers. It is within these contests that there are many opportunities to unravel the carefully devised plans that lead to closing the apparent "trap" of humanity. The pawns do report in the end to one focus of consciousness. Referred to as the "anti-Christ" in literature, he is expected to be born into a human body that is like those of humanity. Unfortunately, that is not true. This "anti-Christ" has existed in the history of this planet and has been the controlling entity by appointment for eons of time. He exists in a form that does not have a short period of existence and might be thought of as immortal. Though painted in literature in various formats of evil, his is a human format, but one of long duration. His intelligence is incomprehensible to the average human mind. However, the character flaw of power is also comparable to his intelligence. Fortunately, he is not the final "word" with regard to the future of this planet. There is a council that has influence beyond his. It is to this council that an appeal must be made. Though he has great influence and through eloquence has kept his controlling influence alive over a long duration of time, it is this council in which greater authority rests.

The question then arises as to how to make this all-important appeal. One or even a few cannot do it. It must be through combined and focused appointment/election of an eloquent and powerful emissary by a quorum of humanity. How can a divided, submissive and victimized humanity ever arrive at such an agreement? Where will this idyllic emissary be found? Indeed, those are the questions! Further, how does this emissary contact and appear before this heretofore-unknown council? It would appear that help is certainly going to be needed to accomplish this. There is help available when the quorum is gathered and the appointment/election is made. First the impossible must be accomplished, and then help will available to assist. This is something that humanity must do in faith. Certainly there is belief in theories more illogical than this firmly held by large groups of humanity. These presently accepted concepts offer far less than freedom from bondage and acceptance of the right to continue on the path of evolvement.

The timing of all these coinciding forces of chance as has

been introduced in previous information, has brought all of this to a pivotal point in the order and process of expansive expression. All possible focus of intent is at work within the factions that are present. At the center of these foci are the dazed and incredulous human beings that hold not only their own future, but the ability to influence the entire galaxy with their decision process. What will you/they do?

III-13

While mankind seems to face accomplishments that are of monumental proportions for a divided and quarreling group that from one perspective is more animal-like than divine, there is light at the end of the tunnel. The ability to continue on the current path is now reaching a point at which the path must divide. There are those who innately know that the time has come to make a decision. They must either continue on the path that is leading to a vibrational decline toward destruction or stop where they are and look for a way to change directions. Herein lies the awakening process. The current choice that is offered by what has been called the "esoteric or new age" alternative lacks grounding in application of its principles within daily life. It requires ignoring investigating and understanding the plan of the planetary controllers for "fear" of supporting them by recognizing their presence and actions. This "head in the sands" approach fails to appeal to the general population for it lacks practical application appeal. Most people are unable to separate their focus to ignore the world around them and replace it with one that they cannot perceive through their 5 senses. This is particularly true because the sources for participation comes from information perceived to be from beings whose teachings recommend disconnection from the apparent real world. Their teachings often are so idealistic as to leave their readers/followers feeling guilty and frustrated for they are unable to attain such levels within their current living situations. In the end, the ideals are abandoned.

It is hoped that these messages contain information that guides its readers to concepts that contain practical challenges that uplift their desire for continued evolvement. It must be understood that this has to be accomplished within the practicality of the experience that is going on within what their 5 senses reflect as their present reality. The difficulty lies in accepting the fact that the inhabitants of earth are not alone in an inconceivably large galaxy. Thousands of visits have been made to this planet and have been plainly visible to extraordinarily large numbers of people for literally thousands of years. It is totally amazing that this has been literally programmed out of the present mass conscious awareness. Aggressive action has long been focused by the self-appointed controllers to block friendly, benevolent beings from direct interaction with humanity at large. This has been stepped up with the placement of powerful military capability into the hands of the human pawns. Again it is important to understand the concept that this is for the purpose of **"having humanity enslave itself."**

As these messages circulate, a distillation process goes on continuously. The information is begun, put aside and then reread. Those that begin and complete it in a flow are few and far between. Reaching this point in assimilating the information has been accomplished by a very few. However, participating in the process in a more leisurely way does not indicate that this type of contribution is less effective. It is accomplishment that is appropriate within the total pattern. Many will never read all the messages. Many will do so in a longer, on and off pattern of participation. It is the composite of understanding that will bring about the necessary changes in the totality of understanding by the whole of humanity that is necessary.

The entire process of reaching the minds, hearts and spirits of those humans who have evolved despite the long standing programs of control has been an ongoing focus of those of greater understanding among your Galactic brothers, sisters and cousins for a long time in your sequential counting. It has taken much effort on their part to create opportunities within the laws that they observe with care to assist whenever and wherever possible. The question arises as to why, if others blatantly disregard those laws, are these beings so careful to observe them? Always remember that the basic law of attraction works in its inimitable way. These beings know this and have no desire to allow their well-earned progress to be eroded in any way by forgetting this law. It may appear that those who ignore or break the Universal Laws that underlie the expression of potentiality into manifested experience gain by doing so, however in the totality of it all, the piper will have to be paid. For those of humanity that follow through on their desire to bring forth this change for this planet and themselves, much will be forgiven through the gift of "grace." This is an opportunity that is to be taken advantage of by those who are wise. The added difficulty of evolvement within such difficult circumstances is being taken into consideration and value added for doing so.

It has been the purpose of these messages to both encourage and lay out carefully a picture that is comprehensible and contains as much truth as possible so that it might be accepted by minds that have been misled and taught to misperceive. That it contains some information that might be less than the total truth is plainly admitted. It was designed to bring its readers forward in an ongoing process of learning concepts and then leading each forward to accept others that opened new vistas of understanding. In rereading the material, contradictions will be found. It is hoped that those that do this will be able to understand the process and realize the purpose and methodology that was employed. The reeducation of an entire population is not an easy process when the basic understandings are purposefully contradictory in a planned and ongoing effort to cause conflict and separation between large numbers of people with incredibly diverse cultural differences.

To conceptualize the problem is to understand its probable impossibility, but that is exactly what the "controllers" are counting on. Let us make every effort to surprise them.

III-14

As the world situation evolves into greater and greater confusion and chaos, what is happening in the larger picture is impossible for the individual to perceive. Each can perceive only that portion of the whole through personal observation and through what truthful media information is available. This is further complicated by the filter of opinion, experience and feelings through which each reaches their own conclusions. Any single person or any group, no matter how carefully known information is analyzed and checked, rarely knows the truth of any situation. As those who would control increase their surveillance through computerized analysis by satellite, scrutiny of communication exchanges, photographs taken in stores, banks and in street intersections, individual lives become documented to the point of infinite detail.

For what purpose is this being done if the abundance of "chemical weapons" would allow the annihilation of all or any portion of humanity at any time? If the human body is being deliberately debilitated through genetic food alterations, additives that are abrasive and destructive, diseases that are deliberately induced through vaccinations, destructive medical practices, etc., to what end is all of this leading? It would appear that humanity is no different than the animals that are demonically used as test subjects for the "good of humanity." What then is to be the recipient of the "good" of the tests in which humans are the focus? In the larger picture, are humans benefiting from the animal testing? Following that thought pattern, would anything of good be likely to result from the testing that is being carried out on human bodies? We again come back to the conclusion that this planet and its human population are but a virtual reality game for those who consider themselves to be superior and in an "ownership" position. We return to the conclusion that someone or some group is misusing their greater intelligence to perpetrate an injustice of great magnitude. The victim/abuser consciousness is being played out on a massive scale.

Surely, it is time that outside intervention by the powers of "good" can intercede. Unfortunately that is not possible within the Universal Laws that uphold all that has manifested from potentiality into creation for the purpose of potentiality knowing itself. All is held in continuity through the immutable laws that govern without deviation. If deviation would occur, all would end in chaos. How then is chaos of any kind allowed? It is here that we must return to a concept that is found within the creation process. Each of you experiences it in your life expression as breathing. Your physical expression depends on it. Without breath, your body can retain life but for a very short time. Within the expression of potentiality into manifested expression for the purpose of experiencing thought into wisdom, there is the necessity of investigating this process within self-awareness by various degrees of knowledge and wisdom. When an experience is complete or reaches a degree of imbalance, then it is necessary that it be dissolved. The energy is then made available to be reused or recycled. This recycling process of dissolving and reusing this energy is called chaos and takes place in the larger reality in what might be compared to breathing. What is manifested, literally comes apart into confusion and returns to energy that is available for reuse. There are as many patterns for this process as there are happenstances of creation; in other words it is unique each time it happens. The degree of chaos needed in order for the energy to be reused is also unique to each circumstance.

How much chaos is necessary for humanity to recreate its opportunity to evolve within a positive situation? That remains to be determined by humanity itself. It is obvious that the current situation has no way to progress without a return to chaos. Those who have evolved and those who have chosen to incarnate on this planet for the purpose of changing the paradigm of experience on this planet hold the key within their conscious determination to play a leading role within this drama that is playing itself out now. The determination of who writes the final scenes for this current theatre production is very much up to those present right now. It will not wait for another generation to pick up the task from another one that has ignored the responsibility and left it to the happenstance of "someone else" to do it.

How much help can be contributed from the galactic community, it must again be pointed out depends on enough human beings rising above the victim focus and accepting responsibility. This is their only recompense.

III-15

As the situation progresses the intensity of the changes that will be experienced by each individual and by those of each culture will begin to become more apparent. Thus far, the changes have affected particular group experiences. However, as the warring factions become more widespread, individual experiences of chaos will expand correspondingly. Eventually there will be more areas of war and aftermath of war than areas of apparent peace. In other words, this experience will spread like a skin disease across the surface of the planet. In using the word war, that includes the usage of biological agents as well as the usual destructive kinds of weaponry. It is difficult to understand what purpose all of this pain, misery and destruction of a beautiful planet can possibly serve. It is in entering the observation mode of the larger picture that the true insanity that underlies the plan of the controllers becomes obvious.

By contemplating the freewill aspect of the Laws of the Universe it would appear to be an element that could return all that is back to potentiality. Indeed it is a possibility! It could be the cause of the end of an experiment birthed from potentiality that would be just another idea that didn't work. It is something to contemplate. However, it is also possible that there is a counter balance for this type of freewill action that upon reaching a certain level of imbalance, an offsetting action is brought into play as a natural effect. If we continue to consider this from the prospective of the virtual reality game, there are always elements of surprise written into the game, not by the players, but by those that formulate the game in the first place. It may safely be assumed that the players in this game did not write the rules. That they are attempting to write new rules is apparent, but those do not supersede the rules that came with the game as brought into being in the first place.

What are these surprises that cannot be overridden by new rules? Those can only be learned by playing the game. That is the point of all of these messages. All the players must play the game and search for the strategies that will allow them to succeed and continue on in the game. The experiences of manifested life are never boring for those who search for challenge by not allowing themselves to settle for what is given them, but strive to create what they desire. However, the Universal Laws must be observed in order that the progress made in the game is continuous in the long run. That does not mean that there will not be temporary setbacks through errors in choices, or that these choices will not be repeated until wisdom is gained through these repetitions.

Thus, we find that humanity has placed its progress in the game of evolution in trusting that these controllers are their "gods" and that "gods" always are benevolent and have their best interest at heart or are fearsome and cruel and there is no recompense that will buy off their wrath. It is time that humanity realize that in order to save themselves and their planetary home, it is time to take up the mantle of responsibility and stand forth in their own power. In order to do this; fear must be put aside. Fear cannot be conquered. Those are words that tie humanity to what has held them in bondage. The very verbiage of the language contains programmed intimidation. Words of war such as conquer, vanquish, threaten, superior, force, intimidate, capitulate etc., etc. keep the focus on competition rather than co-operation. Mankind on planet earth will only transcend this situation when co-operation becomes the by-word of all interaction. Many experiences of a competitive nature can be experienced within the spirit of co-operation, like sporting events, for they promote skills that are of use in other applications as well as in learning to appreciate the capabilities of the human body.

It is contemplating how humans can stand forth in their own power that is the question. This is particularly true when considering the overwhelming organization and power that is being wielded by the controllers and their pawns. However, it is at the basis of this entire situation that the key is found. Humanity has allowed itself to be placed in a position in which it cannot match the opposing forces chosen focus of power. It **must** now find a totally different approach. The one thing that a human possesses that cannot be taken away, though methodology is being developed to attempt to do this, is the thought process. Even those that have experienced mind control techniques involving incredible experiences, are often able to regain their autonomy of thought. It is the combined, co-operative focus on a simple concept that can and will place humanity beyond the situation that now surrounds it and threatens to overwhelm it. It is within the conscious choice to acknowledge the situation, leave victimhood behind and cooperatively focus on an ideal of experience that this power is available to mankind. When a consensus can arrive at this point, then a direct appeal can be made that will bring forth assistance and there will be an end to the current control of this planet. However, the victim/abuser consciousness must be transcended or the process will be repeated until that knowledge becomes wisdom. Releasing victim consciousness will not be an easy transition for it is deeply ingrained within the population of this planet. It is an important element to be held in the forefront of future considerations.

III-16

It has been ingrained deeply within the consciousness of mankind that they are the servants of their "god" of the moment. Over the long space of time since mankind has been elevated into self-awareness those on this planet have been held in servitude and have been subject to the whims of the controller's interactions between themselves. Further, as the manipulated progeny of these same beings, these attributes of contention and competition are a part of this heritage. In truth and reality these deep-seated tendencies of competition and the use of violence to resolve the inevitable friction that results from this focus has served neither the controllers nor the enslaved. Both have remained over eons of sequential time stuck within the victim/abuser mode that has blocked both from evolving.

Failing to live in harmony within the Universal Laws

which includes living in harmony with the natural environment of each home planet leads to the waste of its resources and eventual exhaustion of the ability to maintain life on it. The natural conclusion of that focus of experience is to look outside for another source to plunder. Earth is the source for those who have set that parameter at the basis of their pattern of experience. It is natural then for this same parameter to be the attitude promoted on its perceived colony.

As these messages continue to contribute to greater understanding of the foundation upon which mankind developed within a controlled and manipulated situation, it is hoped that those reading the information will come to understand their situation and their learned attitudes and understandings. In order to change deeply entrenched beliefs and experience, it is necessary to see a clear picture of the present situation. Only then can a true decision be made as to whether this is the path that is desired to be continued or if it is time to stand forth within personal decision and change the course of human history by writing each one's own history and so the history of humanity. For eons of time, each generation has accepted the parameters of experience that has been thrust upon them and waited to be led out of bondage.

It has been said, "when the people lead, the leaders will follow." This has not proved to be true, as each time it has been an isolated group that has attempted rebellion only to be devastated by weaponry that instilled even greater fear within them. This resulted because they attempted to stand forth using the same competitive, war techniques that had been taught them by example. Their purpose was to create an improved version of the life they were leading, with again another "leader" to guide them to a Utopian societal experience. This in truth would have been simply a better version of the usual victim/abuser experience, temporarily. Even if a benevolent leader were chosen, the history of the influence of power in the following familial generations through the competition of the offspring has inevitably led to despotism.

Thus there has been the hopeful expectation that better leadership would be provided by short-term election of leaders from among the people. In this way it was thought that the inheritance of power and the competition between heirs would be eliminated. It should be obvious that this method of choosing leaders has not provided a better solution. Always the people have abdicated their individual power through desiring leadership/government to act as their shepherd or parent. What was desired was a larger experience of the family. A benevolent super being, a benevolent leader, and a benevolent parent, with the power vested in the masculine gender. What has been lost is self-reliance within the balance of both masculine and feminine unique characteristics.

Mankind has little if any faith in the unique distribution of characteristics and talents that if allowed to exhibit individually would bring forth a composite that would birth the desired Utopian experience. At the basis of this experience would lie the spirit of cooperation. The question that arises immediately is how this could possibly even begin within the present situation of separation, hate, distrust, etc., etc. Herein lies the wisdom of the breakdown and chaos that is inevitable when circumstances reach a level at which the current situation can no longer maintain itself. An apple rotten at the core must disintegrate. Thus the comparison is obvious. In the midst of chaos, groups will come together in

cooperation for the purpose of survival. If there are enlightened ones among these groups with understanding and fore-
sight, these can begin a new experiment that suits the members and the group focus. They must not lead, but only advise
and promote the new experiment. If there are enough of these
groups all focused upon this new concept of human existence,
all understanding the history and the need to leave the past in
the past, there is hope for a new paradigm of experience for
this planet.

Difficult as it is to accept, not all of humanity will be
able to participate in the bringing forth of this concept. All
that incarnate on this planet understand this before doing so.
To all, the opportunity to experience manifested reality is
worth the experience of it. Much wisdom is gained and
despite the limited understanding now held by the mass consciousness, is worth the experience. Though humanity
dreams of attaining immortality within the body, that too
carries with it responsibilities that counterbalance perceived
advantages. That known as self-awareness is immortal. To
add to it a body that is immortal includes dimensions
beyond the ability to understand by mind/brains that are not
fully active. It is a situation of first things first.

III-17

As the situation continues to develop, the picture
becomes more confusing from the perspective of humanity,
however from the greater perspective, it appears as movement or change. It is through what appear to be ominous
events that this change begins its motion and in reality
reflects that long awaited momentum is building. This is not

to say that these ominous situations should be greeted with anticipation, but it is important that the observer mode be maintained while also experiencing these events. None of you are asked to be anything but human in your reactions other than to know the truth of what the bigger picture indicates. It is by moving through situations rather than resisting them or ignoring them that experience becomes wisdom. If experience is denied, then the opportunity to gain wisdom is lost.

The knowledge of the history of humanity's birth into self-aware beings, the addition of other families of humans to the mix and the constant interference and prevention of evolvement by the controllers have contributed to the confusion and frustration of those of you who are present now. Without the understanding of who and what you are, there is little hope for change. This is the reason that this information has been deliberately destroyed, withheld, or misinterpreted. The available historical information is presented in different ways because of different interpretations of the documents and artifacts. This has happened partly through deliberate intent and sometimes because of bias and ignorance. It is thus important that more than one source be searched in order that each individual can discern those aspects of truth contained in each. Again the conclusions may vary, but enough of the truth will be discerned by each to reach far more intelligent understandings of the total situation.

What seemed incredulous in the beginning begins to make sense and then allows for acceptance of a reality that has been purposefully hidden to continue the ownership of this planet. With legitimate inhabitants with a level of self-awareness to govern themselves, colonization for the purpose of stripping a planet of its resources is unconscionable. The fact that the colonizers knowingly gave this ability to the beings that were already present on their arrival makes the situation even more objectionable on moral and ethical basis. To further complicate matters, it is the responsibility of the inhabitants to prove that they have the ability to govern themselves and to steward their planet by changing the situation through their own freewill decision. They must discern how to accomplish this within the Universal Laws and, in this case, despite largely not knowing what these specifically are. Most know that the system that surrounds them is orderly and must be to continue, but what supports that orderliness is an unknown. Searches for this orderliness are convoluted into theories of origin that are of little or no importance in understanding how it operates.

The simplicity of the Universal Laws escapes the understanding of scientists who thrive on complications. Simple as they are the diversity and interactions within the application of them cause confusion when the search is for the cause behind the effects. It is so much more efficient to begin with the cause or the laws in their simplest form and then follow their effects forward into experience. The written/spoken enumeration of the laws is fully supported mathematically. It is important to begin at the beginning. The big bang theory does not allow for understanding to be elicited from a holographic process for it is again a search from manifestation back to cause. The diversity available within holographic parameters is so encompassing that to find the cause within its available infinite variety is to be compared with finding the needle in the haystack.

The process of layering information adds to a greater

understanding of the whole in which mankind on this planet finds itself. It builds a holographic understanding that enables those who study this material to change their ability to perceive and discern more of who and what they are and to know more about the controllers. There are many more incredible facts that are available to be known. The question is, "how much is essential in order to bring forth the necessary decisions that will free this planet from the situation in which it is mired?" There is a point at which further information becomes more detrimental than helpful. It is the search for this point that brings forth these messages. It is hoped that commitment and action in the application of the suggestions included will signal the end of the need for more information. At the basis of all action is the transition of consciousness and the decision to answer the call to responsibility that has been ignored and refused for so long by the composite group on this planet.

III-18

The knowledge available to mankind that has been hidden and in many cases buried for thousands of years is rapidly becoming available. The ability to decipher the languages of old and the availability of this information through willing publishers that place it into books, videos and lectures is bringing this to more and more people. The distortions in the translations do create lessons in discernment, but even the distorted information opens minds to the understanding that mankind's history of civilization is much longer than indicated. The evidence by scientists of thousands of years of habitation and the contrast of religious sources maintaining that man has only been on the planet a few hundreds of years has brought forth enough conflict of information to bring any thinking person to wonder about the real truth.

When the information available is considered from the largest perspective possible, the evidence of the presence of the controllers on this planet and their influence in the history of mankind is glaringly evident. The further evidence that their presence has been deliberately ignored and purposefully withheld from humanity is obvious. This is further supported by the "sightings" of craft capable of interplanetary travel that have not only been experienced and reported by people now: reports of it happening all through recorded history have been found by those researchers that have chosen to investigate this area. Personal memorabilia and newspaper reports offer conclusive support. There are too many reports from the past to be considered hoaxes because there was too little exchange of communication to allow for a wave of suggestion to cause imagined encounters.

What puzzles and confuses the average person experiencing the multi-media programmed information being force fed to them is why on the one hand "alien presence" is promoted, and on the other denied at the same time. It accomplishes its exact purpose, confusion. The mind on one hand wonders at its possibility and yet is supported in its denial because such presence threatens all that has been taught over the millennia. The presence of this influence that has totally affected the lives of humanity since before their self-awareness was given to them, has always been the cause of great trauma and mass annihilation of segments of the population. The deception and violence not only of the controllers, but also the inherited and genetically induced tendencies for this within humanity itself, have contributed to slow evolvement. In all truth, without outside influences such as cosmic cycle completions and information such as these messages, the desire to leave these behind and to move forward into creating the opportunity of a new paradigm of experience would not be available for a long time in your sequential counting. The concern and support of humanity by cosmic/galactic fellow citizens have been focused in answer to those who have asked within their prayers and supplications for a longer period of time than most people realize. It is that within the laws, as has been mentioned over and over in these messages, only a certain amount of help can be given, for those who have progressed beyond the level of earth's consciousness cannot give direct assistance without involving themselves within the rescuer/victim/abuser experience. Only those volunteers who are willing to risk for the sake of humanity have made this decision.

Within the confusion of the conflicting information regarding outside presence and its influence in the ongoing history of this planet is the opportunity for the seeds of truth to be planted and to grow into acceptance of the long denied truth of humanity's real history. The information is available now to be gleaned and to open the eyes of enough to the hidden truth and for this truth to spread. Once discerned and believed it can spread quickly and then, as you put it, the jig will be up. The pieces of the puzzle are present, however few have put them all together into a discernable whole. It seems that each is able to focus upon their part of the puzzle, but is unable to look beyond and collect enough of the other pieces to put it together. When those who do glimpse the picture attempt to share, there is not enough knowledge of the true history to provide a background or frame of reference for the picture to be believable or meaningful. Further, there are few that have the skill or desire to look beyond the media provided information and to do the necessary research. It is a matter of whether the information as presented here is believable and whether it will inspire those who question it to look beyond its claims to find out the truth. The valid, documented information with logical conclusions is available!

As repeated "ad nauseum" the ball is in humanity's court. Mankind must be instrumental in the decision and determination of events that will break forever the hold that has been placed on them. The evolvement necessary has been reached by a sufficient quotient to make such a change possible. The cosmic cycle processes to support and boost the possibility of success are present. The information to assist in the process is being made available within the currently available communication flow to awaken and motivate all those that have the opportunity to receive it. How many and who these are is dependent on the continued spread of the information by those that receive it. Is this the only source? Indeed not, however it is what has been made available to each one that receives it. It is your particular source and it is a personal decision as to whether to accept it as truth and also a decision as to its value. Each individual determines whether or not a decision is made to accept an active role and continue its expansive spread. The future of life on this planet depends on these individual decisions.

III-19

The dynamics of interaction between the foci present on Planet Earth are becoming more, shall we say, interesting as the puzzle pieces move into place. Inasmuch as what is actually happening within the holistic interaction is observed in a sequential fashion by those of you that are within the experience, it is difficult for you to comprehend the true progression of the process. This is further complicated for what is known of the true happenings is given only in part and in distorted fashion. Thus humanity is left to grope through the experience. Only through the decision to create a new experience and the further decision to keep the attention focused on the desired outcome rather than the unknowable current situation, an increasing amount of energy will be directed into the manifestation of the new paradigm. As the chaos accelerates those who have the desire for this new "dream" of existence as an ideal or archetype will find it will provide a focus of stability that will become more and more attractive within their thought processes. Their thoughts will migrate toward the pleasant feelings and visualizations that will accompany their desire for this new state of existence. It will provide them with pleasant diversion from the apparent reality that will grow more intense as the chaos progresses toward the point of the release of energy that can then be redirected into manifesting the new paradigm.

The desire to be organized, to get organized, in order to make this change happen will be both assistance and a hindrance in the process. It will be reinforcing in so far as promoting the discussion and awareness of the necessity and desire for changing humanity's long standing status with regard to the perceived outside ownership of their planet. It will also carry with it the seeds of carrying forward tendencies that have in the past prevented true transcendence from the learned pattern of ownership and exploitation of the planet and fellow inhabitants. The desire to organize around a leader rather than around a concept or principle is strongly embedded within the earthly human psyche. The need to have concepts and principle analyzed by breaking them down into minute details diverts the energy of them and allows for divergent trips into dead end ventures. The wasted effort these adventures involve can be limited and often avoided altogether by intuiting the proper direction a focus can follow to reach the intended goal. The process of literally feeling out the direction that is appropriate through imagery also allows for each to ascertain the appropriate group each feels offers greater growth opportunities.

Within the practice of freedom of choice, much progress is available to the individual and this flows outward into the group and to the totality of the whole. It is possible to understand this through remembering the observation of a lake or pond. Bubbles rise from the bottom, each creating their own small rippling effect, yet not disturbing the equilibrium of the totality, but contributing to the oxygenation and enlivening of the whole. Like bubbles, ideas and feelings about what may contribute to the process leading to the creation of the new matrix or pattern add to its birth process. Many will be considered as the proper pieces that will contribute to a balance and harmonious whole and be accepted. Those will change and evolve through participation within the creational expansive advancement of potentiality into manifested experience for the purpose of understanding itself. Through potentiality expressing outward, observing and returning knowledge experienced into wisdom or self-understanding, the diversity of the number of opportunities to pursue within this process is mathematically beyond calculation. Thus the mind is stretched during the consideration of this concept and its possibilities of expression. It then becomes conceivable to realize that mankind has been limited to an incredibly narrow and controlled pattern of experience within unlimited possibility.

As this pattern of experience is purposefully compressed into an even more confined and restricted ability to express, the freedom to evolve becomes even more remote. This greater restriction produces an energy crisis both individually and collectively. This causes the restrictive boundaries to be necessarily more and more heavily controlled. When the number of beings on the planet is considered, it is understandable that plans are laid to reduce that number and that the choices of the intended survivors have very selective profiles. In order to choose these survivors, a great deal must not only be known about the ideal but also about which groups offer the most prototypical candidates. Since the tiniest of details can expand into problems in the future, the genetics are most important in these selections. It is difficult if not impossible for most humans on the planet to comprehend the detail of genetic information that is available now for this selection process. The limited brain/mind cannot comprehend the amount of knowledge that is accessible to the processes of the fully active brain/mind. The potentiality of the brain/mind is in direct proportion to the mathematical odds for the possibilities that are latent within the galactic matrix. In other words, there is virtually no way to calculate the number of possibilities.

In considering this as a starting point, those that read this material can begin to understand the limitations that have been accepted by humanity at this point and realize that it is time to end this enslavement and to claim the heritage available to every self-aware conscious entity within creation. The awareness is the immortal undeniable focus that is free to search for its ultimate expression within the incalculable potential available. That is its birthright. However, how it is to do this is within its own freewill choices. There are holistic levels of self-awareness that are not known to the human mind, and that is emphatically acknowledged here and now. The understanding of this wholeness of the self-aware unit of which the human is a part has been hinted at, but requires an expansion of the brain/mind function in order for it to be assimilated. Access to the necessary understanding of the greater aspects of human experience hinges on transcendence through the victim consciousness into personal responsibility. Again this is a repeat of the theme of lifting the consciousness from the degradation brought about by dependence on dogmatic leadership. It requires the acceptance of standing forth individually and collectively within personal competence and demonstrating the capability of bringing the current situation through the necessary chaos into a positive group focus that will move humanity forward. The potential for this transition is present and pressing to be expressed.

III-20

While mankind is caught up in the delusion of servitude within the belief that the real rewards for obedience are withheld until the end of the lifetime and are to be experienced in another realm, one's personal power is totally compromised. He/she lives in a state of belief that control rests outside of any real personal control. "God" is the ultimate source of all good humans themselves are the cause of all "bad" because of disobedience to some known or unknown laws, rules or regulations that they have broken. Obedience and service are the watchwords of "goodness" which is the "ideal of life." To further add to the ambiguity of the situation, commitment to obedience and service allows for cruel and inhumane treatment of fellow humans at the discretion of religion and government. Within this system, there is no true freedom for mankind to determine who and what they are. There is no freedom to understand that the "God" concept as taught is one perpetrated for one purpose only, to enslave and control beings that have the potential of becoming totally equal to and surpassing the evolvement of those who are foisting this enslaving situation on the humans living on this planet.

Until the humans on this planet are willing to awaken to the illogical data that is presented and understand that it has an underlying purpose, and to accept that it is done for the purpose of control and for no other reason, no progress toward true freedom can be attained. Life for humanity will continue on as it has for thousands of years. The games of manipulation that are in progress now are but a prelude to the events to come. The aptitudes and adaptabilities of the human body and psyche are being thoroughly studied in order to ascertain the future uses which the most adaptable will be expected to withstand. A minimum criterion is being established and only those that meet this will be kept and allowed to procreate. All others are expendable by whatever means are chosen; all of which will be part of the "survival of the adaptable" experiments. As unbelievable as this information may seem, it is the real truth of what underlies the chaotic activities that are happening on this planet. What appears to be chaotic to the participants is a well planned strategy to keep the inhabitants in a state of confusion so that there will be no organization by them to exchange information in a real way toward an understanding of what is their intended future.

It is imperative that a portion of mankind think carefully through these messages and come to see the logic and sense of them. These awake and aware people must then begin to actively share this information with all that have the ability to stretch their awareness to understand and accept these concepts through logical thinking and to begin to become aware that the potential of personal power far exceeds their victim reticence. Further they must understand that this personal power need not and must not be measured in aggressive tendencies, but in the measure of mental, emotional and spiritual focus. It is important to understand that the spiritual focus is not that of the traditional "religions" toward a benevolent or malevolent "God" outside of the Self. Each must come to understand that their power rests in the recognition that each has the opportunity to participate within the consciousness of galactic citizenship that contributes to the composite of how the creative expansive energies of potentiality are directed either toward positive or negative group experience. Unfortunately, this sector of this galaxy has long been caught up within the negative victim and abuser/aggressor experience.

It will take true commitment and focused desire to break free of this well established pattern of experience. It is important to note that the matrix of this pattern has now reached a level of vibratory expression that is at its limits. It is at a point of vulnerability that will allow it to disintegrate into its own chaotic destruction if a new consciousness among its victims were to become well established. It is this goal that underlies the purpose of these messages. It is this change in consciousness that can be the catalyst that can bring about change and the end to the extremely negative experience that has held this planet and others within its web. These messages are but part of an organized effort to awaken humanity on this planet. By opening to the possibility that the information contains Truth with a capital "T" it is possible to begin to find verification of it through other published material. It must be remembered that available information is published through the perception and prejudice of the personal interpretation of the authors. Thus contradictions will be found. Truth can be perceived as existing at the center of a circle with opinion and interpretation focused on it from 360 degrees of observation. It does exist and the more degrees from which it is observed, the clearer the perception of it becomes. It is the openness to its existence that allows for the clarity and understanding of what is the Truth that is grasped.

That mankind was purposefully pushed along its path of evolvement for reasons of servitude are at the basis of understanding the situation the inhabitants of this planet find themselves in at this moment. What must be further understood is that the gift of self-awareness allows mankind to understand they are not limited to this servitude. It allows them to lift themselves beyond this experience into full galactic citizenship with equal opportunity for continued evolvement and participation in the expansion of potentiality. There is no permission from some unknowable super being required. It is your already inherited gift. Each must however, accept the gift and move into the available citizenship and accept not only its benefits, but its responsibilities by first realizing and accepting the true situation that surrounds them and deciding it is time to change it, not some time in the future, but now. There are now available shifts in cycles and other coincidental phenomena to support the necessary change in consciousness. These will assist humanity if the wisdom to take advantage of this perfect time for change is utilized.

III-21

The time to prepare for the adversities to come is now. What can be done? It is imperative that each begins not with the outer concerns but with that which is within. By that, it is meant that each must come into the realization that the attitude and opinions about who and what each one is must be the basis. It must be fully understood that time and consent are the two necessary ingredients to be contributed by each. The time is now and the consent is to accept a total change in the understanding of who and what each of you are. Each is to begin by opening to the idea that virtually all that has been taught with regard to the past, present and future of all of humanity on this planet has been a deception. It is necessary to accept as true reality that which has been told as myth, that which has been denied and what has been predicted/prophesied as the inevitable future. A new foundation must be laid as a basis for the new conception of humanity as wholistic, self-contained beings whose inner awareness is the source of their identity.

The process of changing the reality from permission to

exist from an outside source to personal responsibility is not an easy transition. It requires rethinking most awareness processes. The training to ask permission to literally exist is begun at the earliest stages of development and is presently programmed into virtually every focus of ongoing life experience. Once the truth of the deception is accepted, then the change of belief is met in each day's myriad small decisions. Each momentary choice must be examined in the beginning to determine if it is influenced by personal inner knowingness regarding its appropriateness in light of the new foundation for understanding. The right to personal decision as to what to do carries with it the choice not only as to the appropriateness with regard to the person making it, but also with regard to how the decision will affect those to whom the effects will ripple outward and touch. This requires the acceptance of responsibility with regard to a larger picture. The effects can no longer be transferred to the "power" that formerly was responsible for granting the desire and must be accepted by the individual making the decision. The effects of the decision must be accepted and born by the decision-maker. Thus the acceptance to participate in the creation of a new picture of human experience entails the process of maturation into citizenship rather than subordination to an overseeing entity. Through the careful consideration of this concept it can be seen that acceptance of the disadvantages of "slavery" has also had the advantage of ducking the responsibilities that taking control of one's own experience carries with it.

Just as the settlers/pioneers that followed the discovery of the North American continent by the European countries sailed across unknown waters into unknown situations, so also will the "new awareness pioneers" find adversities to encounter and to deal with on a moment to moment basis. The most important will be found within their own conscious awareness, for it will be there that the decisions will be made that determine the outcome of humanity's future for a very long time to come. The coordination of cosmic cycles that are available to assist in this epic consciousness change will not be available to assist again for a long time in linear counting. The focus of awareness by cosmic/galactic forces will allow the mass conscious decision by humanity to rule its future and turn their attention elsewhere. Earth's human population has this opportunity to mature and grow into greater evolvement, but it will not be forced upon them. The opportunity is just that, an opportunity offered. It must be accepted and acted upon in order to bring about the changes that are available. It cannot be accomplished by only a few, but those few must spread their understandings with concerted effort and zeal in order that the necessary quotient can be reached. It will not be easy. It cannot be put off any longer or left for someone else to accomplish. The window of opportunity will remain open for a mathematically exact time and when it closes, it simply closes. If it does, the future of earth's inhabitants and the planet is bleak indeed. Both will continue to be exploited without mercy. The influence of forces from outside this planet and this solar system underlie all that is happening on this planet. This is a positive given. These forces are legion and are vying among themselves for control. This is also obvious and yet sleeping humanity sees it only in terms of their own small personal experience. The conflicting stories of worldwide activity that reflect these forces at odds with each other are plainly reported even in the controlled media stories. But this goes unde-tected because the larger picture is obscured by deception from the awareness of the most educated and supposedly informed.

The lack of the ability to put all of the puzzle pieces together into a coherent and logical picture leaves confusion as the only available conclusion to all but a few. The necessity to continue to enlarge the picture beyond what even the most informed and analytical minds have done holds the truth beyond understanding. The picture is very, very large indeed. As has been said, "truth is stranger than fiction." Even the most imaginative science fiction writers have not grasped the reality of what is the true picture. It is important that this large picture become known and it can only become known when earth's people, one by one, accept the truth of victim consciousness being the first layer of the foundation that must be torn out and replaced. It must be replaced with the understanding that humans on this planet **are not** second class citizens. Claiming the ownership and governing of their planet is their rightful inheritance. It is their duty and their responsibility.

The planet rightfully belongs to its citizens, not to those of another planet or solar system. In order to control their own planet, earth's citizens must control their own attitude and thoughts about themselves. They must know themselves to be worthy of self decision without permission from other beings or imaginary "god or gods." This requires courage and the ability to respond to challenges. It is in the blood, the mind and the heart to do this if the programming and the attacks on the health of the physical, emotional and spiritual aspects of human existence can be transcended before these do further damage. The results of the decisions to be made by the readers of these messages are critical not only for those doing the reading, but for the future generations of humanity on this planet for a long time to come, if, indeed, there are to be any future generations. This will depend upon which of the vying forces may indeed win out if humanity drops the ball.

III-22

There are areas of focus that the human mind is totally unaware would serve in the change of direction from subservience to freedom of choice. Where the mind is focused determines where the totality of experience will arrive. When the awareness is bombarded with a confusion of ideas and experiences, the holding of a single or singularly coordinated group of ideas, thoughts, opinions and desires becomes difficult indeed. It does not require the effort of what is termed concentration, but does require the broader and more easily managed process of focus. Focus allows for peripheral awareness of events and information that can be noticed and allowed for short-term inclusion without diluting or taking away from the intended direction of the intent of the overall focus. It allows participation within the currently perceived reality while yet holding in the awareness the intended direction of desire, of intended purpose.

Humanity must first allow itself to accept the possibility that it is their birthright to steward this planet and manage their own evolvement without interference or direction from outsiders. Once that possibility is allowed to take root, the desire for this experience will grow within the awareness, for it is well established within the psyche. It is latent, or buried under the mind control programming that has been layered within the social and religious structures on a worldwide basis for thousands of years. This entire program of control (literally) surrounds mankind's understanding of itself like a tough skin. It is necessary to literally squirm within this skin of deceptive understanding and shed all of it in order to perceive and create a new experience. If this were not possible, then there would be no necessity to place so many layers of false information into the minds and to hold it there through intimidation and fear. This need for control at all cost is the clue that the armor is fragile and that the fear of the controllers is far greater than your own. If mankind discovers its power and its true heritage, there is no answer for them but to destroy all but a few and to begin through intimidation to rebuild the population based on the same deception and fear program. Try as these beings have, it is not possible for them to change the necessary DNA programs to reverse the evolvement and return mankind to a more animal like being.

In reality, mankind's saving grace at this moment is the number of outside influences that are vying for control of this planet. Indeed, there is more than one. Is earth that valuable? It is the competition for supremacy that is the important point insofar as the outside interests are concerned. Each has their influenced faction among the deceived. And deceive you they must with clever and deceptive techniques. For those awake and aware human beings, it is possible to perceive these as factions vie for control. Even within the controlled media and religious dogmas there is confusion. Stories are reported, then either changed or withdrawn. There is conflict and competition between various warring factions so that if discernment is practiced the contention and factions are obvious. Many of the visions and esoteric prophetic experiences being reported are nothing more than another form of mind control. When these prophesies include future Utopian life without responsibility, beware. What is important to these factions is which one can win the prize, regardless of the condition of the prize at the end of another phase of history. Meanwhile, mankind has the opportunity to sleep on amid this virtual reality game or to awaken, stand forth in its own awareness and claim the prize, the planet, right out from under the warring factions' noses. They need only to come forth into personal and group awareness of their birthright and collectively stand forth in declaration and ask for help from that point of consciousness and it will be given!

The key is that mankind must evolve to a point of maturity that indicates the ability to accept galactic citizenship. To be a planet of full-fledged citizenship, earth must be self-governed. Otherwise, this planet is considered a colony, available to be owned and ruled by outsiders. Until humanity is ready to be responsible for itself and its planet, it cannot participate in the galactic family. Then it must decide between being a positive or negative expression. Both experiences exist. Difficult as that is to accept, that is how it is. Help is available, but only on a consulting basis. Citizenship hinges on and results in total self-responsibility. It is not a case of aggression versus regression. It is aggression versus progression. Earth has been caught up in the process of rule and control by negative, stuck expressions of the expansive energies of potentiality. If this opportunity to change the situation is taken advantage of, then the decision must be made to simply continue that which has been the victim side of the coin by expressing the other side through aggression and abuse as you have been used, or to indeed create a new paradigm of experience.

As has been mentioned before, when citizenship is a reality through a quorum of humans declaring their independence and self-responsibility, then the opportunity to observe and receive consultation on what other expressions of positive experience are currently in practice will be available. The space in sequential time to synthesize the new paradigm will be given and protection will be provided. Only a framework need be idealized. The proof of the pudding will be in the individual personal changes demonstrated by those humans that are able to shed the skin of manipulation and deception. These must walk their talk, so to speak and live their conviction of personal and group self-responsibility. It goes beyond a change of mind to living the conviction.

Where does one go when there is no capricious god to direct one's wishes, desires and fears toward? Can that empty place that was once filled by the "God" perceived to give and take, answer or not answer, hear or not hear, depending on whim ever be filled again. Indeed! Now is the time to remember the Laws of the Universe and to read them again and to practice them. Each must become the god in their lives, for the laws are the premise of life expression. The messages are written so that each time they are read a different perception is received, more is understood and the desire to experience real freedom is kindled. There is no freedom without responsibility. As responsibility is relinquished, freedom dissolves into slavery, no matter what clever face is painted over it. The choice between these realities, the fork in the road has been reached. It is indeed decision time.

III-23

True to the predictions written into the Christian bible, the false "Christs" abound. Not in the form of people claiming to be "**the** Christ," but in those giving all kinds of "higher" information. Most of this information contains elements of truth. These are people who are most sincere and have no idea that it is arriving in forms of thought manipulation. The elements of truth give credence to that part of each that must have verification in order that the messages are accepted. Much is known as to the way the human psyche functions. The art of manipulation of the mind/brain/body-coordinated functions is well understood. Those that are concerned with perfecting these technologies have much experience in this art for it has long been practiced on beings of lesser evolvement. Because of the free will element and the adaptability of the DNA of humans on this planet, this branch of mankind has proven to be a frustrating challenge to those intent on restricting and reversing the natural evolvement process. The frustration is twofold. Not only does this make humanity difficult to control, but these beings find there are elements of evolvement present that they desire to incorporate into their own life expression. However, thus far, most have not been able to accept the desired changes within their own strands of DNA. Some changes have been accepted, but not the ones most desired by them.

To indicate that the true total picture of the situation in which planet earth is the focal point is complicated and confusing is a major understatement. All players but one in the larger picture have had control of the planet at one time or another. The only player that has not had control is humanity itself. The others want the control of the planet and its inhabitants now. The winning of the competition between them is as important as the prize. Unfortunately, the physical resources of the planet are of more importance than the inhabitants are. Thus in the final confrontations, if the population cannot be controlled, and in order to gain the prize, it is necessary to destroy them, it would be done. Further, considering the technological development of those game players, what chance does humanity have to come through this scenario?

To answer that question, it is necessary to return to the basic fundamentals as given at the beginning of these messages. The 4 Laws of the Universe govern all potentiality in expression. Thus it can be observed that those that vie for the control of this planet have drawn to themselves others that also vie for the same thing. The inhabitants of earth, at this moment, are not involved in that same focus. When and if the inhabitants of earth focus cooperatively and decide to take ownership of their own planet for the purpose of creating a new paradigm of experience, they are removed from the scenario. If they choose to change their perception from victim to self-responsibility for the use of the expansive energies of potentiality, then the picture changes. Each Law builds on the others, and when thought is incorporated within the Laws, it thinks independently, releasing coordinated complimentary actions in ways that cannot be planned by the mind/brain of individuals. For example, the human body was created within the Universal Laws and continues to think for itself, allowing for adaptation that frustrates those with other plans for it.

While humanity is caught up in the games of others and refuses to see itself as a prize in a giant game of one-upmanship, it cannot free itself. It is of primary concern that this picture be given to them in order to see the illusion that has been fed to them for the purpose of keeping them under control while the players continue to vie for overall ownership. The power players are evenly matched; thus each move is so decisive that sequential time is of no importance. The life spans of these players range from virtual immortality to generational changes in which the focus is locked in so that life span length makes no difference to the final outcome. It would be easy for those humans who do awaken and accept the truth of the bigger picture to feel themselves so insignificant as to have little if any power to change the situation. In truth, they are the only ones in the scenario that do have the power to change it. The other players are so locked into their side of the victim/abuser expression that the chances of their changing that perspective are slim to nothing. Humanity has been calling for help, begging the very "gods" who have perpetrated this situation on them, to get them out of it. What chance is there that these beings will do that? None!

The human beings becoming on this planet, if they are to become now, must do this for themselves. They must accept who and what they are, learn of the existence of the basic Laws of the Universe that have been denied them, put them into practice and create their own new expression of potentiality. That is their inherent birthright. There is no other way out of this dilemma that totally surrounds them and in truth threatens their possible extinction.

III-24

As the time for the closing of the cycles comes closer, an impetus is being felt within those who are energetically compatible. Because of the flow of energies that are now focused within the magnetic field of the earth and those thought energies that are available, a mental and emotional discomfort is being experienced by many. These feelings and understandings that something is out of the ordinary are motivating these people to search for a cause and an end to this uncomfortable state. It might be said that cosmic burrs are being planted so as to get the attention of those who are energetically yet outside the level of submissive indoctrination. These are the ones who will find and read these messages and identify with the content and its purpose. The search for the cause and the solution will end with the reading. Then will begin the commitment to a purpose that calls for fulfillment in a way that is difficult to ignore. Once the seeds of a purpose are ingrained within the awareness, it roots and becomes aware of opportunities to express and participate within its expression.

This illustrates the law of attraction as those who are already committed are focusing intention to manifest a new paradigm of experience, the Law of Attraction begins to draw more and more into this shared focus. As the intentional focus gathers more that share this cooperative agreed upon desire, this activates the second Law of the Universe, that of intention to manifest a shared focus. That focus begins to clarify and to intensify, thereby adding more attraction energy. This building of a momentum then multiplies exponentially. It is the shared general point of agreement that is the organizing impetus for the successful manifestation of the intended focus. As the laws begin to act and interact with and within each other, the process of thought thinking begins, thus opportunities and synchronicities begin to be incorporated into the experience of those holding the intended focus in their consciousness. It is critical that those in the beginning phases hold the general intention of creating change through their own desire to do so. Out of this intention will blossom the birth of this new experience. Mankind has been held in bondage and ignorance long enough. There are enough evolved humans present now on this planet who desire to take responsibility for the present and future of this planet to focus this intention into a new reality. It is a matter of getting the truth of the situation into their awareness and offering them a solution that does not require them to sacrifice their life experience to the intentions of other detrimental plans for humanity. It merely requires that they change their attitudes and understand that they are the rightful owners of their own planet, provided they are willing to be responsible citizens of it and of the galaxy of which it is part.

It is necessary that each and all understand that planned manipulation has been foisted on them at every turn, through every institution, be it government, media, societal mores, religious doctrines and the "ground in" understanding that violence and competition are the answer to all problems. Indeed, calm, resolute and unbending intention that underlies all forms of decision, actions and thoughts will bring about more positive changes in one life span than thousands of years of aggressive misuse of each other. Further, it is time to end the allowance of outsiders to misuse the mineral resources and the human/animal resources so generously provided by this planetary home. It might be said that humanity's mining claims have been literally stolen from them through the misuse of these resources on the planet and through the export of them by those who have already misused and mistreated their own planetary home. Now they despoil yours to continue their same pattern.

Careful study of documented information and studied conclusions now available in printed form, leads the discerning individual/group to the inevitable conclusion that indeed something is very wrong. It is time to change the scenario for the sake of humanity and to end the literal rape of this earthly domain that is the heritage and birthright of those whose home it is by birth and by adoption.

This planetary home is humanity's to retrieve and to own, but first the false mining claims must be refuted and correct ownership established. Since the power of the contesting entities for continued colonization of this planet is totally overwhelming, then action of the Laws of the Universe, properly understood and applied is the powerful resolution to the problematic situation that seems so dire when its full picture is comprehended. Through the Law of Attraction, those of singular intent will gather their focus. By cooperatively intending to create a new experiential paradigm of experience, the next layer of power through the 2nd Law will be added and those will interact and integrate bringing forth discernable intensification and expanding attraction of others to the process.

The 3rd Law of the Universe is the most difficult to access and to practice. It is the Law of Allowance. The process must be allowed to construct itself within the focused and agreed upon intent. This law is most perfectly applied through confidence in and acknowledgement of every nuance of manifestation as they begin to be experienced not only as a group, but also especially within the daily happenings of each individual's personal life. The new paradigm of experience is a coalescence of all the individual experiences that fit within the agreed upon focus of intent. These are locked in as they are noticed, acknowledged and appreciated. It is the small occurrences that instill the confidence that is at the center of the application of the Law of Allowance. Doubt is a normal human trap, but when the desire for change is deeply felt and held in mental and emotional confidence, it must manifest. This will not be an easy phase, thus the encouragement of small group interaction with the sharing of both knowledge and "happenings" that support the actual reality of experience will strengthen this necessary application. There are those individuals that will accomplish this phase very much on their own. All are appreciated!

Through the coordinated and integrated action of the first three Laws of the Universe, the 4th Law of Harmony and Balance will manifest into reality. This is not to say that there are no polarity experiences within the Law of Balance and Harmony. Indeed there are, however, there are not the extremes of experience leading to great imbalance. These are merely lessons of discernment that demonstrate knowledge lived into wisdom.

It is the learning to rely on the self-awareness to perceive where each is within the application and understanding of these laws that underlies all of manifested reality. That will replace the programmed need to look outside to some power greater than self for the gift of permission to do something or to fulfill a desire. It is up to the self to attain that desire through the application of those laws for the self and in cooperation with others. Thought properly intended thinks and acts through to completion if properly held in mental and emotional focus for positive change. Focus is "lightly" held by the mind. If you intend for your body to move from one room to the other, it simply does by acting on your intentional motivation for it to do so. It acts entirely within the Universal Law of Intention into manifested action. It is not even a conscious thought, it is an intended action, and it happens. The subtlety of this example demonstrates the power of intention that is "lightly held" but is yet confidently expected to happen. It would be well for this example to be contemplated and carefully understood.

III-25

It is necessary for those who choose to become involved in this process to make a firm commitment to change the perspective through which their life experience is viewed, remembering that the perspective chosen is in accordance with the type of view that is available within each one's personal attitude. This view is either observed stubbornly through a singular, one way only focal point that rules out all other possible choices or it can allow for realizing that other points of view are available. It is possible to think in terms of what is true being at the center of a circle and 360 degrees of possibilities existing. Beyond that lies the ability to expand further into a holographic conceptual understanding in which truth is at the center of a sphere and an almost immeasurable number of possible viewpoints exist. Through this change in attitude, what is known as judgement becomes choices. It allows for others to observe and choose and it encourages the self to quest for more perspectives and a broadened experience. The allowance for other possibilities to exist expands the life experience and brings the being into the flow of expansive energy that is the source of "All That Is" as it understands Itself through knowledge acquired and lived into wisdom through individual experience.

It is difficult to comprehend that each life experience contributes to the composite that differentiates itself so that it can then gather those scattered experiences back into itself in a meaningful way. It can only be interpreted through intelligent beings observing their experiences and drawing conclusions, which is another way of saying experiencing knowledge acquired into the wisdom of understanding. This happens in both separated, individual experience and conclusions as well as group and mass group experience data gathered and processed. The "mind" intelligence capable of doing this is beyond the scope of its finite awareness to comprehend. It is only necessary to be aware that the process is part and parcel of who and what each is. Infinite possibility is constantly being contemplated and investigated. Each and all are the instruments through which this process is going on. Thus it is important to understand there is no "sin" or error, only experience to be lived into the wisdom of understanding and infinity in which to do it.

However, when, through wisdom gained there are those who wish to bring an experience to its conclusion, as do the humans on this planet, then it is possible for knowledge to be made known to those asking so that new choices are available. It is through knowledge gained that the process of asking for assistance is brought forth. However, the asking must be done within the applicable laws that underlie the existence of all manifested experience. There must be an understanding and application of those laws by the requesting group before it is possible to give the assistance.

When considering these messages, it is possible to see the tight circle of circumstance within which humanity on this planet finds itself locked. It is possible to see it as a wheel of existence from which there has been no escape and to understand why those who prefer this planet to remain as a colony rather than an independent self determining unit have employed all possible means to arrange this. Since the actions of these beings are under scrutiny now, it has been necessary to manipulate the population to perpetrate, on the surface, control measures upon themselves, so to speak. Therefore you come to understand the power structures and reward systems that have been fabricated in order to entice those who would apply these control techniques upon their fellow beings as well as instigate destructive functions to the planet for their own apparent gain. How long they enjoy this advantage over their fellow humans remains to be observed. It is to be noticed how often those who have "outlived" their usefulness, and know the inner workings of the conspiracy to control, seem to come to interesting ends.

It is this ability to observe that allows for choice as to what each would intend to have for a life experience. It is this choice process that will enable mankind to change the planned destiny and remove themselves from the control and influence of those who would control and hold this planet as their own rather than allow for its populace to evolve into galactic citizenship. The solution lies in the ability of Earth's evolved human residents to lay claim to their planet by their own recognizance, for unknown to them, theirs is the first right of refusal. Colonization by outsiders is only possible through their permission, in this case by default through ignorance of their own ability to claim it and for the most part ignorance that they are a colony at all. Considering the carefully documented historical evidence of alien presence on this planet for millennia that is now available in print and the myriad of "UFO" sightings, how this foreign presence goes without understanding is illogical and beyond comprehension by all outside observers. It is as though earthlings are totally fixated on continuing to accept slavery and control, except for those few upon which the hope of the survival of humanity and the planet now depends. "May the force be with you!"

III-26

Though the intent and purpose of humanity as a whole cannot be focused as a cohesive unit, a representative group with clear intent and purpose of representing the whole, can set a process into motion. It is the components of intent and purpose clearly identified as representing a whole and focused upon a defined outcome that attract to it the power to manifest into reality. It is the contribution of the many into the focus of a unit of definite intent that draws to it the power of subtle creative energies. It matters not whether the wording of each contributing focus is exact; it is the intent of the final outcome that is the cohesive factor.

For the purpose of example, suppose the final outcome desired is the reclaiming of the ownership of this planet. Suppose a group of those who have evolved on this planet decide that the governing and destiny of this planet is theirs to control without outside interested parties' interference. This would be a definition of intent and purpose that would be clear enough to draw to it the energies of the law of attraction. This would result in those of like desire joining in this expression of intent and purpose in thought. Through the thought focus of this desire and the intent for this to become a reality for the good of the true citizens of this planet and the physical planet itself, the Universal Laws would begin to operate. The thought and emotional desire would begin to attract a greater thought process and energies would begin to coagulate into events and circumstances that would support this process.

The key is not in acting out resistance to the current apparent situation, circumstances and apparent events, but in focusing on the desired outcome. The act of holding the desired outcome within an emotional field of desire for the envisioned outcome is the application of the Law of Allowance. This is the most difficult of all of the Laws to apply, for the events that are happening will still reflect the expression of the established process until the focus of the desired outcome begins to influence the total picture. The process of the two situations must evolve into a chaotic dissolution of the established process before the desired new process can begin to manifest into reality. Herein lies the difficulty, for the focusing group of humanity that is now instrumental in initiating this change into reality is also accustomed to what is referred to as "instant gratification."

Holding this intent and purpose firmly in mind and heart through the chaos into its manifestation into reality is extremely difficult for even those of well disciplined mental capacities.

It is the absolutely desperate situation that is facing the "humans becoming" on this planet and the prospect of the loss of all progress made over these past thousands of years that will be the impetus to do this. To indicate that the above statement is true, it is only necessary to avail oneself of the now abundant material available on the internet, talk radio and many published revelations of conspiracies that subjugate the citizens of all countries through drugs, intimidation and war as well as physical, mental and emotional abuse. The deliberate attacks on the moral, familial and religious beliefs at the basis of human experience are now beyond the logical acceptance of a mind that is not already separated from its ability to logic and analyze data clearly. Fortunately, there remain in the mind and heart of all humans certain keys or triggers that can yet be activated that cause them to click into an awareness state that throws off the carefully programmed acceptance state of the propaganda that has been force fed into their minds. The continued attack on the health of the bodies by the altered food, drugs and medical "health" care system has created a further complication for humanity to rise above. The adaptability of the human body has amazed even the perpetrators of this entire scenario of control. However, the limit of the ability to absorb much more abuse has been reached for many.

It is to be remembered that all of the above is part of not only the planners of the control scenario, but it also plays into the necessary chaos that will allow for the birthing of the new paradigm of experience. Unfortunately, it is to be remembered that nature uses the "survival of the fittest," or put another way, "the survival of the adaptable" as a rule. Thus it is the wise who begin to assist themselves through choice to assist Nature in surviving by carefully deciding what foods and other products are allowed into and on their body, and further, what programming is allowed into their awareness. Almost all media is programmed contrary to the highest and best good of those who regularly expose themselves to it. It does help to be aware of its purpose and decide to take from it only that which serves the highest and best good. It is wise to remember that too much media input overwhelms even the most adept at choosing what serves and does not serve them. Media includes music as well as spoken and pictured presentations.

Those who will bring about this phenomenal reversal of the planned scenario for the future of this planet and its remaining inhabitants will learn and apply well the 4 primary Laws of the Universe. These Laws will become the "god" of their lives and upon the wisdom of these Laws will rest the future. They are the foundation of the new paradigm of existence. All building blocks will be shaped by their application. Their simplicity and the energies and intelligence that their interaction with focused minds that hold clearly their intent for the highest and best good of all will bring forth changes for the good of this planet and humanity that are beyond anything the present human mind can ever imagine. It is the clear and present desire for this incredible experience that must call and hold the minds of all that read and resonate with this information. Upon your mental shoulders rests the future of this planet. The question remains as to whether there is enough commitment and focus to bring about the desire to own and shepherd this planet and your continued progress. A galaxy of fellow god beings awaits your decision and your follow through.

III-27

The question arises as to what others will be doing while those committed to birthing the new paradigm of experience are focused within that process? Except for those who are committed to the agenda of the negative forces, these will be creating the necessary chaos that will allow for change. Therefore, it is necessary that those who contribute to that aspect of the change be released from any judgement on the part of the creative group and allowed to make the contribution that is within their ability to do. Since many of those unable to allow themselves join in the creative focus will be friends and family, this will make it difficult for the "ground crew" to stay focused and to "allow" them to contribute to the chaos. If it can be known and accepted that these may yet be drawn into the new paradigm further into the process, then it will be easier to allow them the opportunity to make their contribution freely.

It is important that those who choose to take part actively in focusing their intent and purpose toward bringing into manifestation a new paradigm of experience clearly understand that making a commitment lightly is not recommended. The material within this series of messages has attempted to educate step by step change in how each perceives the world around them as it is at the moment. It attempts to point out a logical and understandable method by which change can be initiated, but also to state plainly that taking part in changing the intended future of this planet and its inhabitants involves more cacti than roses on the path through the process. The exchange of cacti for roses happens near the ending of the scenario and indeed is well worth the experience. Each is encouraged to remember that once the focus on the desire for a new paradigm begins to coagulate within the mass consciousness, not in quantity of those doing so, but in agreement with both mental and emotional commitment, the Universal Laws of Attraction and Intentional Creation begin to change the total situation. What is happening will be difficult to ascertain in the beginning and will appear in synchronistic occurrences that will not always be recognized. Further, once the momentum of people reading and resonating with the messages and the desire for a new human experience begins to multiply, allowable contributions by galactic neighbors can begin to manifest in further help. There will be those who simply begin to attune to the concept, as it becomes subtly available within the mass consciousness, and begin to add their desire for a new experience without knowing about the messages. Many will have the books given to them or find copies that were not utilized by those who did receive them, a demonstration of synchronistic events that happen through the Law of Attraction as it subtly works.

The thought vibrations as those committed to the project read, reread and discuss the concepts with like minded individuals contribute greatly to the invocation of the Law of Attraction. The power of their intention and commitment then invokes the Law of Intentional Creation and it is further fueled into creative action by the emotions that accompany the desire for this new experience. At this point the person involved has initialized into motion two of the Laws. Holding the commitment and resolve to experience into wisdom this opportunity then leads to the difficult invocation of the Law of Allowance. This requires what has been called "faith" through "knowing" that the Laws are real, do work and are working in the midst of the continued apparent success of that which needs to be changed as well as while confusion breaks down what must change. The heroes, sung and unsung, of the new paradigm will be those who can commit, grasp the understanding of applying the basic Universal Laws and allow them to bring forth the desired goal through the breakdown and formation process. There will be no instant gratification. It will not happen overnight. The plan to dehumanize the population of this planet is too well established to be changed quickly. But, focused desire and purposeful intent can change it! It can only be accomplished by living, breathing citizens who know that they are powerful beings with the Laws of the Universe and the creative flow of Divine Intent that humanity be allowed to choose its own destiny and is deserving of its inherent right to do this. It must however choose its path of self-choice or bow to the overseers who await that choice and do all in their power to influence humanity's decision. The decision can only be made by each individual and those individual choices then meld together into a rising tide of intent and purpose.

It does not matter how much mind control via multiple processes has been forced upon mankind. There will always remain triggers within the mind and heart that can be activated that bring about "changes of the mind" and undo all the programmed responses in a moment. These awakenings are happening with greater and greater rapidity now as a result of many unique coincidences. As the awareness spreads that a new experience is available for the taking by committed individuals, these will increase exponentially. The wave of desire for not only changes, but for reversal of the current trend toward slavery is beginning to manifest. Take heart and do not falter in desire or commitment. The time for the ground crew to redouble its effort and continue on is now. Hold the desire clearly in mind and sense the movement of the Universal Laws as they support humanity and be aware that there are many galactic fellow citizens that are awaiting the time to be of greater help when it is allowable.

There are many cooperative facets that support this thrust for humanity to regain the right to determine its own destiny that are unknown. The ground crews are unaware of each other, however, what each does supports the others and the plan as a whole. There is a plan, of that you can be sure! Just as the oppressors have a plan, there is a plan that does not oppose it, but transcends it. That is a very important difference that is significant to comprehend. What good would it do to simply oppose and block a planned negative experience? It is necessary to transcend it and create that which is new. Consider that concept carefully and remember it in discouraging moments!

III-28

It is to be understood that the time of realization by humanity that it has come to a crossroads is happening now. A decision must be made as to whether to continue on under the influence of those who would continue to control them or to accept the responsibility of choosing their own future. Under the influence of the methods of control being applied now, the consideration of taking such responsibility by a large portion of humanity is not possible. Take into consideration the number of humans who are not even vaguely aware of the situation that confronts the planet and its inhabitants, and the chances of ever attracting the interest of a considerable portion of humans are next to impossible. However. when those who are aware, no matter how few by comparison to the number inhabiting the planet, come together in agreement as to this choice, the balance of power is changed. This is even more powerful when these concerted foci are aligned within the action of the Laws of the Universe.

It is to be remembered that when the action of one group involves interfering with the freedom to evolve of another group, this is in conflict with the natural flow of creative expansion of the galactic/universal environment. A plan that is in conflict with the creative flow requires constant attention and management in order to maintain itself for there is no interactive creative thought to correlate the facets of activity into a naturally cohesive thrust into manifestation. Once the decision is made by a group in agreement to return a deceived group back into the flow of expansive evolvement, "heaven and earth" combine in a flow toward accomplishing that goal. The Laws of the Universe are invoked and "thought thinking" becomes interactive with results that are beyond the comprehension of the originating focused group. The momentum grows exponentially and manifestation occurs spontaneously.

Considering the bigger picture in a condensed version allows those contemplating its accomplishability get a sense of its possibility and grasp a knowingness of how the process works in essence. However, it is necessary that each and all understand that the process does not work by itself. If it did, the situation as it now exists would never have come into being. There must be carefully laid groundwork in order for the process to begin and continue to a point to which it will then complete itself. There is indeed such a point. The originating group will have no way to ascertain this point and so must initiate and continue to hold the desire and intention in place through the greater portion of the process lest they withdraw in over confidence before that unknowable point is reached.

Desire and intention have been stressed many times, however there is action also required. Physical resistance to the overwhelming forces of those who intend to intensify their overseer roles is pointless and futile. Those that intend to change the destiny of this planet and its inhabitants must direct their action toward the spread of the concepts of manifesting the new paradigm. This new paradigm of experience will be accomplished through the understanding and application of the basic Laws of the Universe—focus, intention and allowance bringing forth the end result of balance and harmony. This would appear to be quite simple when considered in its basic conceptual understanding. However, to apply these principles in the midst of coercion, chaos and confusion in a firm trust and knowing that the Laws are working when there is no physical proof to justify that all-important belief is not a simple task. When the 5 senses cannot be trusted to tell each committed individual what is happening, then the process is not simple or easy in its application.

If humanity cannot come up with a group of focused individuals to hold this desire and intention for a new experience in a committed fashion, then the planet itself will begin a cleansing to enable itself to avoid extinction. This process is already beginning. The degree to which commitment is made and held as the subsequent events unfold will determine greatly to what extent the planet will need to cleanse itself. This commitment involves the shedding of the victim stance and the willingness to claim earth citizenship, including the responsibilities that this will involve. There can be no looking back, no blaming for the past and present experience, and decisions will have to be made with regard to repairing the damage to the planet. Greed and abuse patterns must be transcended with the highest and best good for each and all always as the controlling factor. Those who cannot accept these guidelines cannot be allowed to influence decision making situations. Discernment and disclosure of intentions will be the hallmark of all discussions.

If the earth proceeds to cleanse itself, then of what good are these messages and the desire and intention of those who are attracted to this process? Who indeed will survive as a remnant to repopulate the planet? Will it be those who have misused the planet or those who would heal the inhabitants and the planet with loving intent? Since all that exists, as manifested reality, is vibrational, those that exist in a vibratory rate that is harmonious with the planet will find themselves in safe places. Those safe places will exist where these individuals are. There are no "safe places" as designated on the planet despite any and all predictions. There will be safe places in the midst of any and all disaster experiences. It is the consciousness of the individuals themselves that will create those places. Those that respond to the call to planetary/galactic citizenship and are able to transcend the victim stance and take on the mantle of responsibility to create a new experience will come through the days ahead to guide this planet to a new level of experience. The Law of Attraction will bring about its inevitable evening into balance and harmony. Whether any of humanity on this planet presently will come through this experience is entirely up to the choices that each makes. It is the responsibility of the ground crew to offer this choice to as many as possible, as well as to make that choice for themselves and to stick to it as the process continues through to completion.

The cycles are coming to their inevitable completions and the opportunity window is beginning to close. Those beings that have evolved will respond. Those that choose otherwise are to be blessed and allowed to follow their own path. This is most difficult to allow for those connected by family ties and friendship, but there is too much important work to be done to dwell on their chosen future. Seeds planted do grow. Trust the process and keep on keeping on. The future of all depends on the ability to make the difficult decisions of each moment. The emotional strength to do what is necessary is available to all who are committed and who hold the highest and best good of all as their guiding principle. Each is asked to do only that which is the best they can do in the moment and to hold no regrets as to the decisions that are made and the actions that are taken. To learn to trust oneself within each moment to moment experience is to mature into responsibility; a necessary process for sharing the birth of a new paradigm. As each moves through the levels of experiencing into wisdom what is chosen, there is never a lack of the need to exercise courage, vigilance and perseverance. They are the hallmarks of maturity and the signal that completion of a cycle of experience is at hand. Each must decide what point of maturity they have reached and if they are ready to take on a new level of challenge. This is not a project for the faint of heart, the lacking in courage and those without stick-to-ability. Do you know where you are in relationship to this opportunity?

III-29

Within the flow of events that humans experience as a linear sequence or time, the progression of maturation has reached a level of experience internalized into wisdom that allows for a shift in pattern of experience. However, this shift is accessed through the freewill choice that is innate within each evolving human. What is experienced as linear progression, when viewed through the more accurate holographic picture of experience appears as piecemeal contributions to a dimensional whole. Linear observation reflects a flatter, less dimensional picture of progress gained through manifested occurrences experienced into wisdom. In order to comprehend how multiple lifetimes of experience can contribute to the wholeness of their contributions toward harmony and balance within the combined collection of these, it is important to gather them into a comprehensive unit. As the gathering of a unit of experiences nears completion, certain absences of experiential requirements become apparent. Thus certain missing accomplishments are assigned to complete the experiential unit.

A great number of beings present on this planet now are focused on fulfilling their individual requirements for completion or as you might consider it, graduation. This allows the indigenous population the advantage of the infusion of exceptionally talented individuals from various levels of advanced experience to assist their process of attaining the freedom to evolve independently. Who are these exceptional beings? There is no way to know, for they themselves do not know. Are those who read these messages one of these exceptional beings? Maybe! The point is, there is available a reservoir of talent with exceptional abilities. These have specific issues to experience into wisdom and there is no accident that these beings are present on this planet now. Within their knowingness are the need and the desire to complete these experiences. These specific assignments are of value in the birthing of the new paradigm. It is suggested that each reader of these messages search their own heart and mind as to whether their life experience now is a satisfying one. If not, then perhaps within these messages there may be a resonance that allows them to awaken to the desire to fill an inner void that has heretofore been overshadowed by lifestyle, media programming and the general malaise of disharmonious confusion that is proliferating now. It is worth considering the possibility carefully.

The question arises within those who give this thoughtful consideration as to whether those of the other persuasion are aware of the presence of gifted entities? Indeed this is possible and in many cases probable. Many have had their life ended purposefully by the opposing forces. Infiltration is a method used by those involved with both purposes. There is a natural curiosity to know what is going on within the other camp. This is often undertaken by individual choice rather than design, thus one that might appear to be involved on the other side, so to speak, is discovered and eliminated. Therefore, it is unwise to judge all participants as being what they appear to be. Those that have special talent often find themselves within romantic entanglements that lead them far from their specifically assigned experience. These often find there are difficult choices to be made in order to satisfy the inner urge to be elsewhere doing other things. It is to be recognized that the spiritual aspect of self has little to do with the standard religious affiliation that is pushed upon the average person. What satisfaction is found by most has more to do with the victim stance requiring a promise of a rescue connection than in actually finding spiritual fulfillment within the religious dogma programmed into their consciousness. In the search for more understanding of the empty feelings within them they are stuffed with more dogma and misunderstood information, and few ever find true satisfaction except by intuiting beyond the available concepts.

This is not to say that these messages are put forth as a new "bible." This information is for the education of all those on this planet receiving it that can let go of their current literal acceptance of media, religious and familial teachings as well as subliminal programming. This allows them to consider the possibility that there are other concepts and information available that can lead them to fulfill the inner urges that populate their own psyche. There is a greater plan that has been carefully laid in order to answer the long continuing outcry through prayer and thought for release from the stifling hold on this planet and all of its inhabitants, inclusive of human and all other life forms. Each and every human on this planet is a part of that plan. How many will answer the inner call is yet to be known. Freewill choice is the basic rule that can and will be exercised by all. The freewill of those who do answer also includes the measure of commitment and action to spread the information that each allows themselves to do.

The birthing of a new paradigm of experience upon this planet is an exercise in cooperation rather than competition to determine which is the stronger force. Cooperation through focus and intent within the underlying Laws of the Universe has power to manifest that is incomprehensible to the average mind on this planet. The functional brain of humans has had its activity purposefully lowered to prevent the movement toward freedom that these messages are designed to initiate. It is important that those who take this information seriously and intend to become part of the cooperative creative focus also intentionally begin to exercise their mental capacities. This can be done through games, experiential learning and any other method that will separate them from the influence of the media and other "dumbing down" activities that are everywhere in the "modern environment." The brain, like the body, deteriorates if it is not exercised. In order to focus and hold to a commitment, mental and emotional clarity is of the utmost importance. Reading information that is contrary to the promoted dogma and focusing thought for the purpose of discernment as to its validity and the possible intention of the writer is also recommended, including these messages. Much can be ascertained from them by intuiting the purpose of them. Each will, without doubt, intuit different reasons through this exercise.

III-30

Humanity will continue to evolve through the process of

experiencing the changes that are coming through its current experience. By learning of the Universal Laws and how to act and interact within their concepts, the opportunity for rapid progress is present and flowing through the experiences of all who have begun to apply them. When a greater and greater number come to "know" they are true and accurate application of them brings to them the results they desire, then the manifestation of the new paradigm of experience will begin in earnest. It is through their application and understanding with the "knowledge" that they indeed do work along with the understanding of "thought thinking" as they move from focus and intent into real experience the application of them will become natural. It will take no more concentrated effort to apply them on a continuing basis than it does to decide to get up from a chair and move to the door or wherever else you intend without actually applying concentrated thought. It is through intention that it is accomplished as easily as breathing or any other act that is accomplished in the "knowingness" that it just happens easily.

The key to the application is in knowing that the intent must be in harmony with the flow of expansive creative energies that move and carry the manifestation of galaxies, solar systems, planets and individuals through to experience creation in the observation mode. It is necessary to understand that all that is considered reality first begins in the imagination, the mind of the conceiver. The focus of intent moves the process through the various stages of conception to energy conversion resulting in coagulation of that energy by slowing down the vibration until it manifests into observable, touchable matter or what is called manifested reality. What is considered reality is focused intent condensed through application of the Universal Laws by holding the intent firmly and "knowing" that the process works until it does. The slower the vibration of the focusing mind and the surrounding environment, the longer the process takes and the more difficult it is to hold the intent long enough. Learning through application to hold the intent "lightly" without attempting to force its creation but again in "knowing" the validity of the process allows for "practice makes perfect."

There is a great difference in the application and concepts of wanting, believing and knowing. Wanting only creates more wanting, believing only says that one thinks the process will work, while "knowing" accomplishes the intention. It is the degree of difference gained by the actual experience of "seeing" the application work that allows for the "knowing" to become accepted and applied with ease. The first attempts at application must be reasonable and believable in order to reach the "knowable" level of acceptance. The nuances of these concepts are important to contemplate, bringing the understanding that deliberately applying the concepts of these laws may not be an easy task in the beginning. Thus to choose a single application with which to test the theories is of primary importance. It is the habit of man to want everything at once and to fail to take a new process slowly and deliberately. The learning of the application of the Laws is much like stringing beads, one at a time. What is challenging is to hold the concept to be manifested clearly in mind without adding nuances to it that complicate and slow or in fact halt, the entire process because of unnecessary detail. Again, thought thinks and often creates a far more grand application than the finite mind can conceive.

The energies of the individual begin to change as intention and the ability to hold an intention clearly strengthen and hold firm. It would be expected that one or more successes in manifesting a desired outcome would firmly integrate the process into the experience. However, that does not seem to be the case. Most find that old habits and assumptions do not disappear from the experience easily. It takes many successes to raise the acceptance level to create a habit level for natural manifestation. There also are the instances when casual thought manifests as the sub-conscious applies the Laws to these casual thoughts. It is possible to bring into experience instances that apply to others that were never intended. Therefore the statement "of highest and best good for all concerned" is the best possible safety insurance and would be wisely added to all intentions to manifest a desire. A consistent sprinkling of this statement within the continual mind chatter that fills the void between meaningfully aware thoughts is also wise.

To meaningfully apply the Laws of Attraction, Focused Intent and Allowance requires purposeful desire to bring something into real experience. The simple experience unhampered by unnecessary add-on details is possible to manifest quite quickly, depending on the clarity, ability to focus the intention and emotional energy that adds impetus to the creational process. The degree of "knowing" is the final ingredient in the mix. It is difficult to determine the difference between believing and knowing. Again, it is an easy, almost effortless application of the desire, just as you know you can move from the chair to the door. There is an application of the doing of it that is totally without doubt and a knowing of exactly where one is going, but no thought as to exactly what the muscular and other bodily efforts are that are involved, or what may happen during the process of arriving at the door. It is also necessary to continue to "know" one is going to the door all the way to getting there. Losing the focus may allow one to end up in the kitchen and wonder why one is there. In the same way, it is not necessary to delineate what is necessary in order for the desire to manifest. It is only necessary to know what the desire is and to add the minimal amount of focused cooperation that is necessary to set the process in motion while holding the intention of experiencing the desire. It is often mentioned that one needs to be sure one really wants what one thinks is wanted. Most can think of casual thoughts or statements that have brought experiences with consequences not expected. The creative aspect built into all is listening and takes those thoughts and statements literally, especially if the momentary intention is sincere and supported by emotional impetus.

While the explanation seems complicated, the application is quite simple. It is a matter of simply doing it simply. The complicated part is when doubt slows or destroys the effort entirely. To begin by choosing a desire that is totally contrary to the current experience is to set up a formula for failure. To attempt to move from poverty to affluence with one desire is sure to fail. It is best to begin with something small and simple. It adds to the process to act as if the desire is already happening. Place an empty hanger in the closet for the new coat. Make space in the cupboard for a new dish or pot, etc. Then be patient and *wait expectantly*.

III-31

It is through the application of the Law of Allowance that the greatest progress will be made with regard to the invocation for manifesting the new paradigm of experience. This is the most difficult of all the laws to apply for it requires the letting go of detailing the desired outcome. It is extremely difficult for the limited mind to focus on the outcome without feeling sure that it is necessary to also envision the process by which that outcome will come into being. It cannot be emphasized too much that it is the outcome that it is necessary to focus upon. The question then arises within the mind as to what indeed it should "look" like. The fact is the most important aspect to "envision" is what it will feel like. Therefore, it is necessary to coin a new expression such as "enfeel" in order to bring the proper focus on this aspect of manifesting. What is called manifesting is indeed coming into the understanding and the application of the 4 Universal Laws. These have been simplified in concept and renamed to words that bring forward greater applicability for they fit within your normally spoken vernacular. _Focus, intend_ and _release with "enfeeling" to experience "harmony & balance"_ is as simple as it is possible to place these wondrous Laws into your conscious awareness.

It is the intent of these messages to be focused at the planetary level for the greatest healing possible. However, that does not indicate that the individual for their own experience cannot use these Laws. Do remember it would be easy for humans to become so caught up within their own "life drama" that the greater purpose for the planet as a whole becomes lost and "falls through the cracks." The point to remember is that without the healing of the whole, the individual applications of the Law will do little to bring about the freedom of humanity from the planned scenario of control. It is, therefore, imperative that any personal application of the Laws be focused "within" the greater planetary focus. Thoughts regarding this are most productive if all is "seen and felt" within a holographic picture of all applications contributing to the success of the planet as a whole. Within that focus, each individual success in applying the Laws then contributes to and strengthens the greater focus. Furthermore, the individual then draws a greater contributing focus of energy from the planetary whole into their process, a wondrously helpful boost toward their desired goal. Again each is reminded to include the statement "for the highest and best good for all." This releases the "thought thinking" aspect of the action of the Laws to utilize energies that otherwise would not be available to contribute to the whole (holographic) pattern.

The Universal Laws when properly invoked can bring about wondrous changes in situations that otherwise would remain stuck within their current motion and momentum. This remarkable process results in complete re-arrangement of energetic forces that are in motion. This causes a period of chaotic energy shifting but can happen quickly *if* it is released (allowed) to complete the process without the input of imposed restrictions to its motion by the "intender" by continually adding thoughts to the process on how the Laws must bring about the desired focus. It is this necessary release/allowance that is the key. The educational process has brought mankind many blessings, but it has also allowed for great limitations. The simple tribal experience with faith in guided rituals often brought about remarkable changes with success based on previous experience and allowance of "unknown" energies to bring forth the desired change. It was the allowance of that "wise" outside energy to accomplish the feat that allowed it to happen. How much better it is to understand that the "outside something" is but the naturally existing Laws that underpin all of existence acting through the focus and cooperation of the mind/s involved.

It is also important to mention again the added impetus that is gained when more than one mind agrees in basic concept on a desired focus. It is possible to "know" that the agreed upon desire for a new paradigm of experience can be the encompassing focus. It is possible for it to contain myriad individual foci each contributing to the success and fulfillment of all when the "highest and best good of all concerned" is the releasing factor. The greatest success is accomplished when the foci are concerned with the outcome and not the how, why, when and ifs that the human mind is so good at conjuring up to contemplate. It is this unneeded contribution that "gums up the works and throws the monkey wrenches" into the process. This not only slows the process but can cause it to fail to manifest or worst of all bring forth a convoluted version of what was potentially possible. Thus, it is again stressed that the discipline of holding the focus on the desired outcome is of the utmost importance in allowing the process of the Laws once set into motion to bring into manifestation that which will serve the greatest number to their highest and best good.

This message will need to be read and reread in order to help each to keep in mind the exactness required in laying the foundation for the successful application of the basic

Universal Laws. The habits of the undisciplined mind are deeply ingrained. However, practice followed by success and holding to the simple repetition of the basics over and over again will bring about the desired new paradigm of experience. The holographic concept of all fitting together within a matrix that contains infinite variety within a whole can and will allow for the freedom that mankind yearns to experience.

It will be necessary to incorporate these concepts within the mind and the heart in order that these become the new "god" that each finds necessary to fill the void within. In this way, mankind can at long last come into the understanding that each is an expression of the Divine Order that is "God" knowing Him/Herself, All-ness in Self-contemplation. It is necessary to further let go of the need to "personify to identify" this greater concept of "God" and accept it as an on going process. Consider this carefully.

III-32

The empowerment of humanity is of the utmost importance in the outcome of the entire scenario. This empowerment cannot come from the outside. This is an inside job that each individual human must accomplish on his/her own. This is not to say that there is not guidance available to trigger and assist. These messages are the perfect example as are the comments, articles, books and all other triggering phenomena that are available to accomplish the awakening of each and all. The overload of media availability to many of the current world inhabitants serves the awakening purposes as much as it does as a mesmerizing tool. It takes constant reinforcement to keep the lid on conscious awareness.

However, sudden discernment can cause all of the cleverly layered programming to fall away and understanding to instantly awaken when the proper triggers are activated. A simple statement that makes total logical sense within the thinking/nervous system connection causes a realization to register through out the awareness and in that moment there is a change in the ability to receive thought that has hitherto gone unheard and unnoticed. It is this process that is the purview of the "ground crew."

The agreed upon focus of the "ground crew" involves the awakening process as well as the primary focus of the desire for a new paradigm of experience through "outgrowing" the victim experience and accepting the responsibility for changing the human experience on this planet. All who respond to this challenge are capable of accomplishing it, or the goal would not have appealed to each in the first place. The "Johnny Appleseeds" who plant idea seeds are "heaven sent" to do this. Consider carefully this idiom of speech. Many common sayings, when heard in the new context of change, have been speaking to the consciousness of each for a long time. Those will henceforth have great meaning and will trigger consciousness changes as they are noticed. The awakening process is ongoing once it is begun. Like a good mystery story, one clue leads to another in an ever deepening commitment and synchronicities will become a way of life. Chance comments, a word, a story line, a news note, etc., all will fit into a different context than previously. Particular friendships will have greater meaning and others will diminish in importance as the focus of interest changes.

The work, the focus of what it is necessary to accomplish, will redefine the thoughts and the available time. A natural realignment to what is important will change with little direct attention as far as the personal life is concerned. When the focus and the intent are upon the outcome being for "the highest and best good for all concerned," it will happen of its own accord. What will be accomplished depends upon the strength of the foundation set forth in the very beginning. The simple statements of intent such as "help for all humans becoming" and "for the highest and best good of *all* concerned" set that foundation upon a firm and level beginning for they broaden the focal point beyond the personal scope while yet including it. The globalization of interaction and activity by humanity at this time no longer allows for experiential change to be limited to a country, a continent or a hemisphere. In order to accomplish the transcendence of humanity on this planet as a whole, it was necessary for there to be an inclusive global consciousness. Until this was possible, change was only piecemeal and easily destroyed from within as well as through direct intervention by those who plan to continue their control.

In considering the picture from a linear event observational mode, timing seems inordinately important. Within the understanding that a picture of wholeness can be filled in by events and circumstances that do not appear to be happening in a sequential mode, it is difficult for those participating to ascertain and comprehend the larger picture. Without understanding accomplishments as they fit within the bigger picture, it requires great self discipline to hold the desired outcome firmly in intentional focus. It is because the increasing inflow of newly awakening awareness requires those of greater understanding to constantly redefine the purpose and the intent. This then in turn refreshes and renews their own focus.

From an energetic pattern point of view, this provides for a spiraling of greater available dynamism. It is the entry of more and new awakening awareness that provides this important momentum and allows for a continued increase of available energy that offsets the inevitable fallout of those without the ability to maintain their commitment. Many of these will be drawn back into the activity and again provide the addition of needed impetus. As the focused pattern begins to clarify and increase in momentum, its drawing magnetism will begin to be felt within the planetary mass consciousness.

It is when the pattern begins its clarification and its energy begins to draw from the negative focus that the greatest difficulty will be encountered. The assumed superiority of that group is unquestioned in their minds, thus they feel little if any concern about the attempts being made by organized groups to change the perceived future of earth and its population. It is the lack of organization and the emphasis on individual change and participation that does now and will continue to allow the transcendence of consciousness to reach the momentum and pattern clarity necessary to change the synthesis of the mass consciousness. Once this point is reached, then the methodology as employed by them to control large segments of the mind of humanity will erode quickly, provided the momentum can be maintained.

Indeed, critical points will be reached and must be moved through. It is then, in answer to focused and deliberate requests, that outside help can intercede in subtle ways that will assist in moving through those crisis moments. "Help to become" will be answered. Thought thinking will provide the exact needed assistance. It will not come as intervention, but as assistance. There is a very important nuance in the different meanings of those words to be contemplated and under-stood. There will be no mass invasion of extra-terrestrial ships to rescue humanity. That would not allow mankind to work out its own solution to the dilemma in which it is now embroiled. At all times, humanity must create its own solu-tion to invoking a new destiny story. There must be no mis-understanding of that fact. Victimhood and galactic citizen-ship are two opposite poles of experience to be understood and deliberately chosen. This is done by way of myriad small decisions and actions as experienced on a daily basis by indi-viduals in their own life experiences. These experiences then gather their own energy pattern reflecting a larger experience by an *intentionally focused* group of humanity. That is what will bring about the changes so greatly desired, prayed and begged for by suffering humanity through this long and dif-ficult period of its history.

III-33

This is the sequential period of time that is the leading edge of the chaos that has been mentioned many times in these messages. The pattern of existence as it has been known on the planet in recent millennium has begun to dis-integrate. As in all cases of disintegration, portions of the coagulated (manifested) energy do not dissolve, but tend to break into pieces that become destructive to the portion that remains intact. In order to understand this; think of energy in a formation that resembles a lovely snowflake. Picture it as made of a sturdy material and see in your mind's eye por-tions of it breaking into pieces and being tossed about and causing other portions of the pattern to break down from the impact. Since all manifestation consists of solidified energy, this is a reasonable comparison. Once energy is solidified, it does not return to its origin (light/thought) without being broken down by the same creational process in reverse. However, that process is not an assignment for this ground crew. The larger picture that encompasses the totality of Earth and its inhabitants transcending the currently planned future contains many separate foci in order to bring the new paradigm of experience into being. It is only necessary that as much understanding of the process as it is possible to explain and is helpful be included. It is more important that each segment of the whole focus on the portion that is their agreed upon assignment.

While all are curious about what the "big" picture looks like, it would indeed be impossible to explain. It is to be remembered that as "thought thinks," nuances of change can cause major differences in outcomes. Because freewill is a major component in the process of creation and allows for diversity within wholeness, the mediating factor within the working of the Laws of the Universe is the ability for thought to think *within* the whole. In other words, "thought thinking" can consider all nuances of change throughout the whole and compensate for effects that the finite mind has no way of considering. It is the wisdom that evolving consciousness strives to emulate. The Laws of the Universe are totally compatible and cooperative. When the Laws are invoked, and intent and purpose are in cooperation with them, there are never disagreements or discussions as to what, how, or which method or approach is right. It is simply done in the most advantageous way! There is no ego involvement as is present in situations of less evolved thought processes. It is these ideals that are sought in the dimensional progress of evolving consciousness. As these are mastered, each progressive life experience provides for new and different challenges to be lived into wisdom.

Presence on Planet Earth in these times is not and will not be lacking in challenges. Opportunities to live challenging experiences into wisdom will abound. Those who can focus their intent and purpose to take advantage of these opportunities will benefit greatly. That is indeed a glib statement that in the moment has little meaning. However, if when others are in panic, one can "keep his/her head clear" and listen to the "knowingness" that is available to all that will listen within, decisive action will prevail in the moment. It is a matter of taking that second or two to listen/feel what is the appropriate thing to do. It is a skill that is acquired by practice. Applying it now in the small decisions that are made each day can provide practice. Much is done by mere habit. As the situation changes, those habitual actions/reactions may no longer be appropriate. It is important to begin to pay attention to the thoughts and feelings, especially those that reflect apprehension or concern. It is time to begin reprogramming the conscious awareness to be more and more active in moment to moment decisions. "To do or not to do?" That is the question to be asked within each conscious awareness. It is of utmost importance that these questions are asked of the individual self-awareness rather than asking others for their opinion. Only the individual is experiencing the decision and is in the situation: the decision may require action in brief moments. Through practice, confidence and trust with that inner knowing part of self will be built.

Becoming involved through commitment to the "ground crew" requires focus of intent and purpose. It also carries with it the advantage of connection to a flow of energy that is purposefully aligned with the Universal Laws and the flow of intelligent thought that supports creative expansion of thought into matter. This connection involves a balance of responsibility and compensation in direct proportion to contribution. It does not reward foolish input that endangers the outcome. Development of the "feeling" of appropriate words and actions is a prerequisite to wise participation. The major portion of the process will be accomplished by individual awareness and consciousness change along with dedicated intent and purpose to create the desired new paradigm of experience. It is the focus on the intended outcome through "knowing" the desired outcome can manifest when participants are in harmony with the Laws and truly desire "the highest and best good for *all* humanity on Planet Earth."

It is to be expected that as the influence of this focus of intent to change the planned destiny of mankind begins to affect circumstances and situations, the usual method of destruction will be employed, that is to infiltrate and destroy from within the organization. However, there will be no organization to destroy. No doubt, individuals will be "removed" from the focus, but there will be few if any records to indicate what individuals are responsible for the change taking place. Once the triggers change the conscious thinking process of those participating that will be the only connection that can be made, on a one by one basis. Meanwhile, the spread of the consciousness change will continue with its inevitable results.

Thus, the purposeful intent to structure the change within the individual consciousness serves a dual purpose. It increases the opportunity for individual evolvement and provides the vehicle for the advancement and transcendence of the planetary whole without the danger to life and limb that would be associated with the usual rebellion scenarios that have been repeated over and over to little or no avail. The advantages are many, most of which are yet beyond the limited human mind to comprehend. That too will change. With the acceptance of self and planetary responsibility, the brain/mind will activate to a greater and greater degree. Though purposefully imposed, the limited brain capacity was held in place by the victim consciousness. That in turn was held in place by the desire to be rescued by a source outside the self and humanity as a whole. This further provides the understanding for the weekly programming lessons stressing the need to ask outside help in all areas of life, to turn over life to outside greater wisdom, and the media depiction of the constant stream of victim situations. All is carefully coordinated to keep the victim consciousness firmly anchored within the mass consciousness. It is our purpose to change the mass consciousness to personal and planetary responsibility, where it belongs!

III-34

Within the blessing of education, the proliferation of broadcast communication and the printed word for the distribution of knowledge lies the problem of discerning what is of value and what is deliberately placed within these sources to mislead and misinform. Herein is the next level of understanding that discernment as to what is appropriate and true must be applied to all input. Within each is the source of such guidance. The ability to tap into this wisdom is present within all and latent within most. The lessons in learning to discern what is appropriate and what is not are many and frustrating. For most, these are trial and error with difficulty in figuring out what purpose experience serves in life. Once the concept of discernment is understood, it is learning to use this important tool that is at the basis of many of life's trials. It then becomes a useful tool that enhances experiencing knowledge into wisdom.

It is to be understood that discernment is a tool that replaces what has been called judgment. Each can then release the self-deprecation that comes from "judging" self and others as being right or wrong. Discernment is an internal process that eliminates looking outside of one's self for the cause of the seemingly difficult experiences that plague the human life. The dictionary lists "insight" as an appropriate synonym. Discernment can be applied in a before or after mode. It is wise to consult one's inner feelings carefully before undertaking an experience. It can be further applied in retrospect to understand what lesson can be gleaned from an experience that is happening or has happened. Unless a lesson is learned, it is likely to be repeated until it is "discerned." Then a realization of what the intended lesson is/was happens within the understanding of the individual or group.

The practice of discernment is part of the application of the Law of Allowance. To consider the appropriateness of an undertaking in either the before, during or after mode requires a letting go of the emotions involved in the experience so that the logic of it can be considered. This may be an ongoing process of consideration before the totality of the lesson is gained. Even partial understanding and realization of its purpose in the totality of the life experience allows for greater knowledge to become wisdom which in turn allows the individual to apply this and change their pattern of expression to include different possibilities. In order to consider the situation and its circumstances there is a letting go that is necessary in order to allow the mind to consider the possibilities of the who, what, why and how of the total picture. If there is considerable open mindedness, possible scenarios can be played out in order to determine the greatest number of possibilities. Through this process, the more logical meanings become clear. Through this release needed solutions often become accessible because the mind has been allowed to reach inward to access the available wisdom from within. Each has a storehouse of available wisdom that is obtainable through the practice of discernment. There must be a desire to lift personal experience out of the daily morass of pointless repetition, judgement and blame.

In order to shed the victim consciousness the individual must be willing to turn their view of life from looking outside for the cause of situations and circumstances to looking inside for the causes that invoke what the Law of Attraction has brought into experience. These causes are to be found within attitudes, opinions and self-talk, for the mind is speaking within in a constant flow of chatter. Within this internal conversation are the keys to many of the patterns of thought and behavior that set up the situations and circumstances that are being experienced. Changing these patterns that are the basis for the creation of the life pattern is not a simple task, but a good beginning can be made with the awareness that it all begins with discernment. The world does not just happen to anyone.

It is invited through the Law of Attraction, for like attracts like. A victim attitude draws not only fellow victims into one's life, but also abusers to provide the victim experience. As each begins to accept the responsibility that the cause is within their own pattern of experience, and is willing to accept this idea, then the practice of discernment is possible.

The discerning individual will find it necessary to logically assess their attitudes and opinions. Are they judgmental and blaming of others? Are there always reasons that the self is not responsible for what is going on in the life experience? If so, then denial of personal responsibility is blocking all progress and the cycle of victimhood is established. Until such time as this can be looked at with logic and the pattern discerned, it remains locked into the experience. It is necessary to desire to change these basic controlling factors, look and listen to what is thought and said and purposefully change the basic pattern. The results will take time and diligent correction in order to see the changing pattern in experience. However, the pattern must change if the intent and purpose are held in focus and thought and words are changed. Statements made can be restated in a positive mode, this then changes the first statement. Thoughts can be "re-thought."

Simple as this message content is, there are few if any who cannot find application of these ideas in their daily experience. The practice of discernment is an ongoing focus through many levels of experience. Looking within at attitudes, opinions, statements and thoughts often reveals interesting and applicable causes. Each is encouraged to apply these suggestions in an ongoing fashion.

Discernment is further practiced in considering and choosing what information is true. It is a wise practice to set up the discernment process by stating in thought that one wishes to discern truth before listening, watching or reading. In that way the mind discards what is not true and retains what, if anything contained, is true. What is truth for one is not always truth for another. Each pattern of experience sets up a different ability to glean what is necessary to know. It is encouraged that this suggestion be used when reading these messages.

III-35

As the sequence of events seems to accelerate and lineal time to pass more quickly the chaos will grow. Each individual will experience their own sequence of events that are only a small portion of the total picture. The controlled media will report only segments of the true picture. When viewed from the perspective of the planetary whole, there is a far greater degree of chaos now present than can be perceived by humanity. Those yet in zones of calm have little frame of reference for the experiences of those who are in the midst of war, geological or weather phenomena. Though greater global awareness is present, yet there is little exchange of actual experiential trauma between these separate experiences. It would not serve the planetary wholeness if there were such a connection so that all were experiencing the trauma of those within the distressed areas. Those that appear to be uninvolved serve to hold the equilibrium of the planet steady as the chaos is experienced elsewhere. There is a balancing that takes place.

It is planned to increase the experience of chaos in order that this balance may be forfeited. This plan to deliberately upset the balance by increasing the chaos beyond the planet's ability to retain its balance is based upon the theory that once the imbalance reaches a certain point, it can be pushed into a negative vibration that will block its access by positive energy foci. In other words, the planet would then be wholly owned by those of negative energy vibration and would then be no longer accessible by those of balanced or positive energy vibrations.

In order to accomplish this it has been thought that it was necessary to lower the vibrational fields of the inhabitants to a point that survival of some would be possible when the conversion to pure negative energy is completed. The installations of massive energy converters in order to bombard the ionosphere have been planned for this purpose. The testing of these converters appears to be for reasons other than what is planned. Indeed they are to "protect" the planet from positive foci and appear to the planners to be accomplishing their intended purpose.

The question remains as to whether the theory on which all of this is predicated is one that will produce the desired change of polarity and if it were applicable, what are the implications that would accompany the result. When change is undertaken within the Laws of the Universe, the "thought thinking" principle can and does work through all the possibilities and probabilities and reaches a conclusion as to feasibility. When change is attempted without this inclusive aspect of wisdom, there is the inherent danger that unknown factors are disregarded and the outcome is likely to be unstable at some point in the process. This then brings the situation to the consideration as to how far freewill can be allowed to operate if the use of it involves massive risk to whole segments of creation.

Freewill with regard to individual experience is inviolate. However, when "will" is focused into a situation that is for the deprivation and destruction of not only the freewill choice of evolving consciousness, but to the point of destruction of the soul energy at the basis of life expression, then careful consideration must take place as to how this situation may be handled. The situation not only demands consideration and decisions, but also involves the decision of what intelligent foci may be involved in making that decision. In other words, a stacked deck cannot exist either for or against the continuation of the experience. This creates a considerable dilemma in coming up with a consortium of qualified and empowered "beings" willing to become involved in such a situation for serving in this capacity puts their own evolution at risk. Evolution is in reality a growing participation in responsibility. It is not a movement to a Utopian existence of lesser involvement or fewer responsibilities. Just as maturation into earthly experience naturally involves greater participation and responsibility, so also does evolvement into the higher dimensional realms.

A great "talent" search was initiated in order to find a cohesive group willing to consider the dilemma that the situation upon this small planet contains. To say that it covered a great deal of manifested reality is an understatement. The vested interests in the future of this planet are varied, well established and of intensely determined purpose. At the irrefutable basis of any solution is the will of the human population on the planet involved. It is then self-evident that those who would retain their control of the planet would make every effort to make sure the inhabitants "decide" that change is undesirable. Herein lies the purpose of the massive release of communication devices and the focus on the retention of the victim consciousness. The foundation of victim consciousness has been carefully laid within the religious foci from the very beginning. It has allowed for control of the progress of mankind not only in the discovery of the "god-like" qualities that are inherent to all, access to the understanding and application of the Universal Laws, but also to the understanding and ability to relate to the "creator mind" that is available within the outflow of undifferentiated energy at the basis of all Creation.

The key to the entry of the gathered wisdom foci is held within the collective mass consciousness of humanity. Unless the individual and collective desire of humanity for freedom from the oppressive outside intervention that has been present on this planet for thousands of years is focused toward an end to this situation, it cannot and will not change. The only possible help that can be given at the moment is to focus energies into the available thought realms surrounding the planet in the hope that individuals will accept these subtle suggestions to augment the desires that are already there to bring forth a change within the collective thinking of mankind as a whole. This seems like drops into an ocean of misery, but in accordance with the freewill principle, nothing further can be done.

The presence of craft from positive origins, what are called extra-terrestrial visitors, among those of negative and earthly origin as well as visible energy patterns imprinted on the surface of the planet has been increased. It is hoped that these will stimulate curiosity and trigger into awareness some of the volunteers that now risk their level of evolvement in service to their fellow humans. These messages are received and circulated by individuals that are responding to this plan. Those of you that hear of these, read and respond to them are in reality coming into harmony with the energy of concern and the desire to assist that is being generously focused into the atmosphere surrounding earth. The electrical charges that are being forced into the energy fields encircling earth are being placed there in an effort to block all positive support for the planet and its inhabitants. Fortunately, all efforts in harmony with the Laws of the Universe are supported by the intelligence of "thought thinking" which finds ways to circumvent such plans. If mankind can indeed be triggered to desire its freedom, despite the plans to block any such assistance, then the Universal Laws can and will support them. However the focus is to be held on that which is desired instead of retaliation and resorting to the old methods that have failed to bring mankind manifestation of their desire for change in the past. In other words, the focus must not resemble that which it is desired to leave behind.

The human population that desires to experience the opportunity to evolve in freedom from oppression must focus on what is desired and let go of the experiences of the past. These have led them in a continuous circle of repeating what has been taught to them by the example of their oppressors. The same blood/DNA of those oppressors flows in the blood of humanity. The question remains as to whether there are enough humans on this planet that have evolved beyond those genetic aberrations that do not serve their advancement. Can they focus on the desire for freedom from the repetitious pattern of life as they know it and transcend it into a new paradigm of experience? Can they now live those experiences into wisdom?

III-36

When each individual being incarnates on this planet it is with the explicit intention of blessing all experiences into wisdom, not only for themselves, but also for the planetary whole. It would seem that each individual life expression can hardly be a blessing to the planet and its inhabitants as a unit, but that is very much the case. Each has the opportunity to focus her/his life experience for the "good of all concerned." That inclusion is far reaching indeed! When this intention can be coupled with harmonious application of the Universal Laws a great contribution to the planetary consciousness is made. Fame or fortune need not accompany this contribution. Most often, the greatest contributions are made in obscurity and often without the conscious knowledge of the person doing so. These individuals simply experience life as a pleasant and harmonious sojourn. These are often recognized as being an "old soul." A term applied to those who seem to create for themselves an experience of simplicity and contentment and no recognition is given to them as accomplishing anything in particular. However, from a larger perspective their contributions are a major balancing factor.

This does not in any way take away from those that do place themselves in the forefront of activity and contribute greatly to the focus of attention to not only great "good," but also to great "evil." It is difficult to consider that those that focus evil into recognition are of service to the planetary whole. It can be considered that they draw to them the evil that is present in the mass consciousness as a boil draws the infection present within a body to a crisis point so that it may burst or be incised and removed and healing may take place. It is the tendency of humanity to judge and blame individuals and situations from their individual point of view rather than from the larger picture of planetary wholeness. Each has their own particular purpose for reincarnating and through the Law of Attraction bringing into experience what is needed to complete the purpose for the lifetime. As mentioned previously, each lifetime is a contribution to a greater totality of experiencing into wisdom. There exists a holograph of experience that requires the completion of various segments of experience in order that completion may be experienced.

Therefore it is unwise for individuals to decide what is good or bad with regard to the behavior of others as well as their choice of lifestyle. Each is to strive to accomplish what seems important in the moment and to listen to the inner guidance that is available to all. It is difficult to do this in an environment of coercion at all levels and periods of life experience. Fortunately, there are those that do hear and/or feel strongly what is appropriate for them and consistently move toward their unknown goal/s. Frustrating as it is, it is one of the requirements that the goal/s are either forgotten or are influenced out of the awareness by the parent/religion/government influences present from birth until death.

As each moves through their sequential life experience it is impossible for them to ascertain their success or failure with regard to attaining the intended goal. Each must follow their guidance and keep on keeping on. A life filled with synchronicities and one that answers inner urgings to undertake what seem appropriate actions and that appear to accomplish the desired goals may well be on "track." This is especially true when the ultimate purpose is for "the highest and best good of all concerned." This may be stated in other ways such as "creating a win-win situation in all ways possible," etc. It is the intention that is measured! Through ethical intention the first two Universal Laws are invoked.

If "ethical" is a prerequisite, then why indeed does evil seem to succeed? It is because the Laws work regardless of who employs them. It is the outcome that is measured by the ethical intention of the "highest and best good of all concerned." The intended manifestation process that is contrary to the "good of all" must reach a crossover point where unknown instability destroys what is not harmonious in the larger picture for there are no individual minds capable of interpreting all possibilities. It is the clarity and duration of the intended focus that does hold a "evil" situation in manifestation beyond the normal point of destruction. Knowledge of the Universal Laws is not normally an unknown. Therefore, those who plan to hold onto Earth as a colony know and understand their application well. It is the human population that has been denied the knowledge and understanding of them so that they cannot use them to help free themselves from the plan to continue their enslavement. It can therefore be understood why the knowledge of these important laws is a prerequisite to those humans calling forth the freedom of Earth's inhabitants.

These messages have from the beginning been leading the readers toward the acceptance of the Truth that they contain. It has been necessary to slowly and carefully lay a foundation of understanding that moves beyond blame for the condition in which humanity finds itself. It is important that mankind accept the responsibility that they have allowed themselves to be duped and misled over thousands of years to be the slaves and toys of those who would control them. The plan to hold them in this deplorable condition has been one carefully implemented since man has been allowed to "rule himself." That these human rulers were/are carefully controlled is absolutely true. By absenting themselves, the true rulers have hidden their influence behind blind faith augmented by cruel punishment for disobedience meted out by "a God of love." The paradox of this claim has kept mankind in a constant turmoil and exactly where it was planned that they be. It is the hope of those waiting patiently for evolved humans to see through the ruse and to declare among themselves the intention of ending this practice once and for all. It is the key to all hope for creating a new paradigm of experience.

III-37

It is essential for the ground crew to understand that their commitment is to assist humanity to take advantage of their help and the opportunity of the completion of the various cycles that are reaching their culmination. The outcome beyond that is to be allowed. Indeed those members of the ground crew that participate will sink or swim with the human population on the planet. However, in lifetimes that are yet to be experienced the rewards for this work will be experienced if the effort to free those on this planet fails. Those members of the ground crew that do not answer the call to complete their mission will indeed become part of the destiny of the human population. It is the risk that was known to them in the beginning of this process. The degree of the opportunity available depends upon the participation of each individual. In no way is this intended to be a threat but as encouragement to look carefully into the inner awareness as to the validity of these messages and to "feel" what is the appropriate response. Participation within this phase of the plan is not appropriate for every human. To become aware that there is a plan that can lead to freedom to evolve can then lead these that do not fit into this particular focus to diligently search for their proper place within the effort to birth the new paradigm.

Humanity stands on the brink of what is opportunity or disaster. Those are blunt words, but it is not to the advantage of an entire planet to mince words and walk softly. The process is proceeding according to both plans and a convergence point is looming in the not too far distant future, as it is experienced in sequential time. Those in awareness must focus and direct their intent to participate and to involve as many as possible within their focus of intent. Tomorrow is not soon enough to begin.

What has been known and experienced is what is expected to continue in at least a somewhat familiar format. This will not birth the new paradigm. Atlantis, whether believed as real or as a myth, is an example of this. The story that is known is of a continent containing a greatly advanced civilization with a well developed scientific community and a very strong religious priesthood that controlled the development of all phases of the civilization. Though there were survivors, most of these were reduced to what is termed "caveman" status for their tools of advancement were lost under the sea. The stories of "how it was" became mythology within a generation. After the passage of several thousand years, what now exists in comparison? Again a well developed scientific community that is controlled behind the scenes by religious and supposedly "esoteric" brotherhoods. Behind these in reality are the extra-terrestrial true rulers making sure that their colony stays under their control. The reduction of mankind to utter poverty of physical and religious experience failed to allow them to maintain a destiny of continuous enslavement.

Unless a focused portion of the population is willing to take on the responsibility of deliberately intending to change the repeating cycle of apparent advancement followed by the return to poverty of body, mind and spirit, nothing will change. The age-old question of "Why does God allow this if He truly loves his beings?" rises to the minds of humanity over and over again. The answer is always the same, freewill! If self-aware beings choose victim consciousness, the Law of Attraction will provide them with fellow victims and abusers to maintain the experience. The desire to move *through* the victim experience thus experiencing it into wisdom with the intention of creating a new paradigm of experience for the whole of mankind and this planet is the purposeful intent that is necessary. This must be held in the forefront of all thought regarding this process. Will this salvage the planet and all of the human awareness units on the planet? Only those who are willing to participate. Who these will be will be decided within the soul matrix of each individual.

Participating in life experience at the 3rd dimensional level blocks from the understanding the activity of creation that goes on in the higher dimensions of experience. These underlie or support those of the lower vibrational levels of existence. Life is often thought of as becoming more focused and rising to a point of completion resembling a pyramidal experience. Using this example, it is necessary to understand that the pyramidal experience is supported by focused thought that may be understood to be its energetic counterpart, thus creating a double pointed structure. That which is seen or experienced is supported by an energetic format of focused thought and these interact on an ongoing basis. If this thought format were to be withdrawn, the manifested portion would cease to exist. Each human life is supported by an energetic focus that holds it in format. Each mountain and grain of sand is held in focus by its energetic counterpart. To illustrate this principle within the life experience, a business or organization is held in experience by the thoughts of those who participate by their focused thought. If that is withdrawn, it no longer continues to exist. It continues or it fails based upon the factors required and whether or not these were included in the focus of attention and intention.

The information contained above can be carried over into the previous discussion of placing attention and intention within the application of the basic Laws of the Universe. By releasing them in harmony through proper intent, the action of the "thought thinking" function of the Laws can and does supply the factors required for true manifestation of the desired outcome to the highest and best good of all concerned. If the intent is held firmly in mind and heart and at the same time released and allowed to manifest through the action of the Laws, the outcome will assuredly be harmonious.

While the information contained herein is often repetitious, it is written so that each may be convinced that there is a way out of the ongoing repetitious cycle of experience into a different adventure. Life fully embraced leads to wondrous adventures.

III-38

When the time arrives for each individual to make the decision as to whether these messages are in fact guidance indicating what their mission in this life may be on this planet at this time, a resonance with this greater objective will fill the void that has been felt within. Recognized or not, until each identifies what their particular dominant purpose is, there is a need to search and find it. This leads to physical changes in location, career changes and frequent visitations to various churches as well as other community and athletic endeavors. Often times it necessitates fervent participation within a focus that does not satisfy the empty the need in hopes that more of the same will eventually be fulfilling. Mankind has been denied the understanding of how to commune with the greater aspects of that part of him/herself that has placed their awareness into this life experience. This aspect is alluded to in religious literature but with little meaningful guidance. Meditation is taught, but the overload of media input along with the stressful life style of "modern" life seldom allows most to reach a point at which the mind is able to free itself to reach the quiet point required to commune with the focusing aspect. It is as though the brain cells are stimulated to an operating mode that cannot slow down to a resting point of awareness. In this state of stimulation, the thought processes do not function normally. The thoughts are not comprehended and considered and are instead, simply processed through. This then accounts for what is often referred to as the "dumbing down" of the modern day mind.

This frantic mode is further pictured in life styles that

reflect constant busyness through hurrying from one task to another. Relaxation is musical noise, TV, movies or videos. Sleep is induced with alcohol, sex, drugs, or late night eating resulting in exhaustion of the body's functions. Simple quiet time such as sitting to observe a sunset and contemplating the joy of being alive, of counting one's multitude of blessings is seldom done, even by the older members of the current culture. The learned busyness is continued until disease or infirmity demands a slow down. The point to be made here is that those who choose to participate in this focus of intention to create a new paradigm of experience must realign their priorities. In order to create something new, a separation from the attachments to the old must be eventually made. That does not say participation must be given up, but their importance must be allowed to diminish. In order to contemplate what is new, there must be quiet space within the awareness to do this. Priorities must change to allow for slowing down the participation in meaningless endeavors and a greater peace sought through choice. Quietness must be redefined from boredom to peacefulness.

Seeking peace in proximity to urban noise, airwaves filled with unseen but very present vibrations and living amid crowded visual surroundings is challenging. Artificial light inhibits the ability to observe and enjoy the evening twilight and the view of the star filled heavens. What countryside is close by is also filled with exterior lights. Work schedules continue day and night. The planet itself has extensive areas of constant activity that further exhausts the wholeness of the global entirety. Is this purposeful? Indeed, for it separates humanity from its connection to the planet that nurtures it and prevents mankind from reciprocating in any way. Humanity at large is on a "taking binge" with little understanding of the necessity of a return flow of energy to the planet through appreciation and honoring the provisions that maintain life.

How then do those who accept this change of focus come into balance and harmony with the global whole in order to enhance and magnify their presence into a focus that will augment the necessary transition? The way is through applying the Laws of the Universe within their own experience. It can be done through intention and attention to what choices can be made to bring as many peaceful moments into each day as possible. The Law of Attraction will work when the attention and intention are clear. Time off from frantic activity, even a small space of quiet time, can have a "grounding" or quieting effect. Positive prayer that centers on appreciation and blessing of the self and others rather than on what appears to be lacking in life will change the experience. Who one thanks is of little importance, for this again is the need to personify and identify. "The power that Is" is sufficient identification. It is the thankful "heart" (feelings) that is important. One cannot expect to create a more abundant experience if one is not appreciative of what is already within the current experience. By honoring what is, the Law of Attraction is invoked.

Thus it is important to find positive attributes in the current experience to appreciate and honor even as a new paradigm of experience is desired. This is the paradox that is found throughout creation. In order to have what is new, it is necessary to honor aspects of what is present as a stepping stone on which to stand before creating a new stepping stone to continue the progress. To honor something does not make it necessary to carry it on into the next phase. Again it is necessary to point out that the grateful heart reflects a feeling aspect that resonates with the Law of Attraction that brings into experience more for which to be grateful. It is the way it works.

III-39

As the sequence of events begins to accelerate, it is time for those who are committed to the change of experience for humanity on this planet to seriously focus on the idea of the realization of the new paradigm. In order for it to manifest into the reality of experience, it must first become real in the minds of those who identify with this idea. It is rather like pulling the proverbial rabbit from the hat. The event as seen requires focused intent "behind the scene" and a great deal of practice in focusing on this desire in order for it to appear. The event itself is a manifestation of the intent that precedes it. What appears as a magical event to the observers involves instead focused practice and the intent to mystify and surprise. There is a direct correlation to the birthing of the planned new paradigm of experience. The new paradigm will arise out of the "grass roots" desire of humanity to end the current descent into slavery. Under what appears as complacency and ignorance of what is going on in the life of the "average" person is the feeling that "things are not quite right." Beneath that awareness is a cognition that is sending forth a signal calling for balance and harmony within the planetary experience. This psychic signal is the platform that provides for the creation of the new paradigm. It is upon this critical foundation that those who read and identify with these messages have permission to dream/imagine the framework that will begin manifesting into reality the desired new experiences.

The key to the survival of this focus lies in its lack of organization. There is nothing to infiltrate and nothing of substance that appears to support its existence. But exist it does! It exists in the minds of growing numbers of individuals and answers untold uttered and unuttered prayers to countless ideas of divine power that is believed to possess the ability to intervene. In truth, it is the manifestation of these prayers and the underlying desire for balance and harmony that is coming forth as the "messages" and the focusing of these through individual minds into the mass consciousness. This is then the answer to these "prayers" and desires. The divine intervention is manifesting through those who desire it. The invocation is made through thought and is being answered in like manner. Since thought is the impetus for all creation, the invocation and the answer are in the most powerful and yet subtle form. It is also the most defensible when it is firmly held and emotionally powered. No amount of subliminal influence can alter the emotionally held conviction that is focused upon a desired manifestation. Desire, firmly held in mind with emotional knowingness that the possibility of its actuation is feasible, can and will manifest. It matters only that the perception that is held by many is *generally* identifiable through statements of purpose.

Those who are now actively involved within their own focus with or without a small group have now reached a quorum to allow the invocation of more help from outside sources. Meditations/prayers and simple thought requests are encouraged to be directed to request help to assist humanity to focus on a different experience as a solution rather than on the problematic situation that surrounds them. Greater awareness of the problems serves to promote an awakening from ignorance, but in no way provides for a solution to those problematic situations that are enumerated. Indeed that which is hidden behind the problems and that invokes them is organized with intentions that are deeper and darker than can possibly be ascertained from the currently known situations. The hoped for return to prior known experiences would in no way hold these dark intentions in check. It must be clearly understood that all hope must be focused toward the invocation of a new paradigm of experience. The past must be allowed to become the past. The future must be imbued with the hopes, plans and dreams of harmony and balance within the application of the basic Laws of Universal experience. It is the shift into this tried and true method of manifestation that will provide the solution to mankind's dilemma. It is through focus on what is unknown and yet to be discovered that the present is let go to become the past and that which the future can offer is discovered.

What is unknown conjures up either excitement or fear. It is important that the ground crew builds upon the emotion of excitement and anticipation in order to provide greater potential for manifesting the new paradigm into realized experience. That which begins as the nucleus of the intention will then draw to it what is necessary to bring about the maturation of the original idea and allow for the what might be compared to cellular growth and expansion of this idea into manifested reality. What begins as a small focus of intent then expands from within and can be promoted further by help from without. The available help can offer protection which enables the natural expansion to continue rather than be contained by those who would prefer that this intentional focus be aborted or die in its infancy. It is this kind of help that it would be wise to invoke during prayer or meditation or focused thought. It is "help to help yourselves" so to speak. It is requests for help to open up the path of mankind before them so that it can be seen and understood as it is experienced into reality. That kind of help fits within the Laws of Galactic Citizenship to be exchanged between its members, freely asked for and freely given. "Help us to help ourselves!" It invokes no indebtedness between members. It is the way of advancement in which all that can, help all that ask, but those must be willing to help themselves in the process. It cannot be done for them. The means of help is left to the helpers for often generally worded requests for help are filled from a greater understanding that brings forth results undreamed of by those requesting it. Greater thought thinking is always available to answer requests formatted within the basic Universal Laws. Thus requests including "for the highest and best good of all concerned" invokes this greater wisdom with extraordinary results guaranteed.

It is hoped that those who identify with these messages and intentionally change their objective to bringing forth the new paradigm of experience for mankind on this planet will remember to hold this focus in the forefront of their attention. The principles contained are of course available for application within personal experience. It is strongly suggested that dedication toward the planetary whole is the basis upon which the individual experience is focused. To change only the individual experience will not change the planetary experience. However, changing the planetary experience is guaranteed to change the individual experience. Both can and may be coordinated by those who truly desire to take advantage of a time that is ripe with opportunity for rapid evolvement. There is much to be understood and the choice involved is momentous for mankind as a whole and each individual that chooses to be consciously involved. "Pray" (think and ask clearly) that enough make the correct choices and purposeful application of focused intention that the highest good is manifested for all concerned. (To *what or who* this request is directed matters not.) What is the highest and best good for both individuals and mankind is an unknown. Judgement withheld _allows_ the 3rd Universal Law to wield its powerful influence. The coordinated action of the first three manifests the 4th, harmony and balance, the essence of the goal of the new paradigm humanity desires to experience.

All begins with the consideration of possibilities, then choice. Choose carefully!

III-40

Circumstances, situations and events are perceived through the sequential experience pattern of the earth plane through a reformatting of a greater experiential matrix. It compares somewhat to unraveling a knitted sweater into a long thread that only retains the individual kinks that made up the stitches. It is impossible to ascertain what the sweater looked like from the pile of kinky yarn that is then seen. Thus each event in the sequential chain of events is all that can be perceived of an existing prototype that is whole and complete. Once the experiential chain of sequential events has reached a completion point of its cycle and a reality is experienced as complete, a perspective of the entire event can be glimpsed. However, it is only one perspective of a holographic whole.

The concept of time that is the basis for perceiving sequential events exists and is experienced differently within each level of manifested reality. With the ability to perceive a greater and greater perspective of a whole, the importance of minute by minute time calculation becomes less relevant. What becomes important is the encompassing process that contains the situation or event as it is completed into a whole experience. It is like watching the sweater being knitted as a whole from freshly spun yarn. As it is knitted, it becomes the background for the embroidery of individual experiences. The same sweater background is perceived and embroidered by each individual who is living within its influence. Each sees their version of the sequence of events, situations and circumstances that then makes up a larger and larger group experience as perceived by all from a myriad of perspectives. The consensus of the group perspective then becomes the "mass consciousness" experience. Out of that generalized agreement, laws, rules and regulations govern what is generally acceptable behavior. It is this consensus of acceptable group behavior that is so important to the oppressors to influence. The more uniform and regimented the world population is, the easier it is to influence and control through identity in a "global" perception rather than within cultural, ethnic or national allegiances.

At the same time as the globalists are attempting to standardize the human life experience into a robotic and more easily controllable worldwide situation, the human psyche is longing to individualize. The larger view of this intense struggle between containment and creative expression is beginning to clarify into groups of varying experiences. A large percentage are being slowed and standardized into a hypnotic zombie like existence. Others are caught up in frenzied accomplishment of various extremes of life experiences. Some are lost in various group foci that exploit their fellow humans, etc. Underlying the whole chaotic scene are the mind manipulators that carry out their influencing experiments on their human sacrificial guinea pigs. Mind programming, medical experiments in the form of prescription drugs and vaccines, illegal hard drugs, food additives, food combinations, unseen vibratory waves from commonly used communication devices, appliances, etc., all influence the human body and the vibratory/electrical spark of life that animates it. These conveniences provide seeming comfort and ease and are thus difficult to think of giving up. It is not the concept of them that is counter-productive to human experience, it is that they have been designed in a planned format that is intended to accomplish very specific negative goals for mind manipulation and control of body functions. In other words, all these beneficial items can be made within a format that would support the life forms on this planet. It is important to understand that these were designed purposefully to slow and confuse the vibratory life force that inhabits all living forms on this planet with the direct objective of eliminating all but the most resistant that these may then breed the most adaptive future slave stereotype. Mankind must come to realize that just as they have thought nothing of doing genetic breeding of life forms that

Becoming

they considered "lesser," so also are they considered a lesser life form by those who direct these human lackeys to misuse their fellow humans. Those who allow themselves to be used in this way are given no more and probably even less appreciation than the average human. If these will betray their own kind, then they are truly untrustworthy and that is not a desirable characteristic for a slave archetype.

It is important that as many open-minded humans as possible come into the understanding of just what their true status is insofar as those who consider this planet their colony are concerned. This is not meant to cause any re-evaluation of the worth of humanity to a lesser value. Indeed not! Humanity has running through its veins the blood, the DNA, the potential of all self-aware beings to evolve within the plan of creation. What is important to grasp is that humanity faces the enviable challenge of throwing off the yoke of outside influence and facing up to taking responsibility for creating its own future. It will be through growing to accept this challenge and creating a way through this experience that the true autonomous qualities that have been deliberately forced into a latent state must now be called forth and brought into focused application. These are not the warlike tendencies of competition that have been cultivated and encouraged, but those of responsibility, courage and cooperation that will bring about the spiraling of evolvement into galactic citizenship. These will lift the human consciousness out of the seemingly hopeless struggle that surrounds it and allow the planet and those inhabitants who change their perspective to transcend this present situation. Those who identify with this new paradigm of experience will move into it. Those who do not, will be allowed more experience until another opportunity is created individually or collectively to choose again. Advancement is available to those that choose carefully and decidedly. Again, each is encouraged to consider thoughtfully.

III-41

Since the beginning of the time that this planet was inhabited with warm-blooded mammals the process of evolvement toward self awareness was the goal. This is a normal and natural process. What is measured as time by this self-awareness as it progresses and is refined appears as short segments in what appears as a long process. Again we refer to the holographic picture of the whole process. The linear sequential observation of the self-aware ego has no inkling of the larger picture until such time as explanations of "how it really is" can be placed within his/her perception and are accepted as truth. The convenience of the light and darkness cycles as a measure of time determines the perception. However, there are other means of measuring time that can be adopted. The longer the cycle measured the longer the life experience of the individual. Though it might seem impossible, were another measurement adopted, then the life span in actuality could be either lengthened or shortened depending on the content of the cycle. How could this "content" be compared? Not easily by the participants. The point being that the experience is conditional on the criteria for measurement used by the observing egos. These are agreed upon through the generalization of the input of the many opinions of the total group.

This is a powerful tool to control insofar as manipulating a large group is concerned and explains the grouping of people in cities and the efforts of using mass media methods to shape the generalizations of opinions. Some of those now shaping the generalizations are:

Power and permission are in the hands of an outside deity.

Violence is the way to resolve differences.

Humans are more different than they are similar.

Being right is more important than understanding.

The past controls the future.

Pleasure and luxury are the necessities of happiness.

Complexity is more satisfying than simplicity.

Might makes right.

Service and sacrifice are the ultimate gifts one can make to the future of mankind.

There is not enough and those that have must take it away from others.

If it isn't "right," laws and regulations can fix it or more control is the answer.

The list could go on and on.

What is it then that the messages found in these small books would replace as currently held beliefs:

Responsibility and freedom are interchangeable terms.

Power and permission are retained or given away by choice.

Purposeful *focused intention* is an all-powerful tool.

What is believable must be logical.

Responsibility negates victim/abuser attitudes.

Where the attention is, is where the intention is.

Like *attracts* both sides of the "likeness experience."

There is an important distinction between indifference and allowance.

Humanity has a choice about its future experiences.

Rescue without participation is not an available option.

The new is invoked in kind before the end of the old.

Chaos is a necessary stage in the process of change.

Commitment to a goal attracts assistance to aid its completion.

Through the reading and the rereading of these messages, these and other principles toward the choice of choosing the destiny of mankind on this planet will become a deeply rooted focus of intent by all those who choose to be a part of this process. It is logical and it is one focus that can be participated in by those with many divergent views without the necessity to defend or attack the diverse thoughts the new paradigm invokes. The "desire for a new paradigm of experience" is all-inclusive. The intent focused for the "highest and best good for all concerned" allows for *thought thinking* to bring forth an organizing agreement that will profoundly include all rational possibilities into an encompassing plan that will be readily acceptable. Humans becoming will indeed become. It is a focus of energy that is all-inclusive and yet extremely discriminating as to choice for participation. It offers the long awaited opportunity to mankind to transcend its colonial status for sovereignty and participation within its galactic community.

The question arises now as to how long before those who desire this planet to remain as a colony will allow this to go on providing the humans of earth to free themselves through declaring their sovereign ownership of this planet? That is a part of the plan that is well encompassed. It is first and foremost the job of humanity to make its choice and to declare their intent within their own awareness and commit to assuming the necessary responsibility to focus their purposeful intent into the Universal Laws and allow the picture to clarify. Thought thinking is wise indeed! Some things are better left to resolve themselves through allowance. However, remember that allowance is not indifference, it is watchful observance with emotional expectation anticipating the outcome of purposeful intent. It is change through conscious participation in expressing the principle of Life that is known through the gift of self-awareness. It is found by perceiving what is known and felt within the feeling aspect of awareness through logical consideration of questions asked within the thinking process. It is thought thinking within the individual consciousness and testing its conclusions through the feeling aspect as to their validity in quiet contemplation knowing there is no need to compare the conclusions to any one else's process of decision. With no need to defend the conclusions, true contemplation is available. The consensus is important only to the contemplator. Think about it!

III-42

Through the process of broadening the perspective of the human experience it becomes easier to identify with the task of changing the intended future experience by returning the controlling focus to the beings evolving originally on this planet. Each unit of awareness that incarnates (experiences in a body) on this planet identifies with the past genetic history of that body as passed on by all the previous progenitors. This then carries with it the right of sovereign ownership of this planet, not as an individual, but as an individual part of the family of humanity. It takes little review of the past history of "royal families" to see the pattern of behavior that is present within that segment of the mass conscious memory. The review of history in light of the influence of those governing directly or in manipulating the members of humanity that were chosen to fulfill that role points vividly to greed, deceit and treachery as standard operating procedure. Indeed, there is little of enduring value to be gained in repeating the experience of humanity in this past chapter of planetary history other than to create a deep and abiding desire to transcend it into a totally new pattern of evolvement. This is not to indicate that there has not been a great deal of progress and much experienced into wisdom. It is meant to indicate that all that is practically possible to learn has been gleaned and it is prudent to release the need to continue and to move on to a more rewarding pattern of experience.

As the consciousness shifts to allow a more encompassing view of the human experience, a different way of perceiving the content of the mass consciousness allows the observer to more easily perceive and acknowledge the influences at work that are deliberately programming the overall attitudes and opinions that shape it. The observer begins to separate from those influences and to recognize them as being forced on those that would not knowingly choose them by outsiders of another nature with a different pattern and focus. This recognition then leads to a choice as to whether to purposely continue within this pattern or to separate from it in purposeful intention to bring about a change for the whole of the planetary experience. To attempt to separate and maintain an individual focus accomplishes little of value whereas joining a larger focus of intent to change the planetary experience offers a solution of enough value to incite a commitment. As has been mentioned before, a change of individual expression does little to change the experience of others, while a planetary change will affect all individual experiences within its scope.

These messages continue to follow a theme of clarifying the current situation with its probable continuity for humanity in a downward spiral of experience into abject slavery and the intended destruction of the soul energy that is the focus that places and holds the spark of life within each body. That spark is experienced as individual self-awareness. Stripping this aspect of life from the human expression would return it to the animal state and to what is thought to be an ideal slave archetype. That is the simplest explanation of the planned future. The greatest problem is the desire of the controllers to retain a percentage of intelligence that is linked to the self-aware state. Thus, experiments and continual testing go on to determine what techniques of mind control and physical adaptability can bring about this ideal prototype. It is hoped that this planned scenario that awaits those who continue to accept the indoctrination, the vaccinations, the regimentation and the subordination of their will to powers outside themselves is now vividly envisioned by those who read and accept the possibility that the content of these messages contains truth. It is hoped that the logical sense of bringing about change by a method not anticipated by those that intend to control this planet and its population is clear. It is possible to change the experience by conscious choice and by deliberate intention through aligning that intention with the basic Laws of the Universe. These bring about deliberate empowerment by allowing the Law of Attraction to release requested help to assist rather than to rescue. At the basis of this plan is the essential change in the perception of the situation at hand and the change in consciousness from victim to responsible creator of a new paradigm of experience. Releasing all of this into the flow of creative expression is the desire that all happen for the *highest and best good of all concerned!* It must be understood that this is not to be intended for beleaguered mankind only, but all that are involved in the entire scenario, whether they appear to be of positive or negative intent. Within that desire to encompass the greatest possible change in experience lies the greatest possible empowerment for transformation in the galactic experience. It is a moment in this segment of galactic history that is unprecedented! It carries with it unparalleled opportunities for evolvement to those who have the desire and the commitment to become an active participant in this shift in consciousness. It is hoped that many will be able to change their perspective and to encompass the possibilities that are available to contemplate. To knowingly be an active participant in this opportunity is even more phenomenal. Consider this opportunity carefully.

III-43

The process of lifting the mass consciousness out of its long-standing morass of controlled attitudes and thoughts concerning what it is necessary to experience as a human is progressing toward a shift in focus. It is necessary that there be formed what might be called an enlightened or knowledgeable nucleus. These messages are intended to serve that purpose. As these are read and reread, those that resonate with the information contained within them form a pivotal core for the attraction of greater numbers to join the growing momentum toward the creation of the new paradigm of experience. To desire change is one level of involvement, but to desire change within a feasible format that is based upon a logical sequence that allows for a group consensus of agreement brings about a momentum that has within it the promise of success. As the momentum begins to build within this focused core of belief in the success of the process that is now well initiated, it is not experienced by these same individuals seeing the actual results for those are and will continue to be unknown from a practical sense. It will be experienced instead as an inner knowingness that all is working exactly according to plan. Though mankind has long sought to observe and control as many aspects as is possible within their life experience, in this case it is known from the beginning that it is necessary to "trust the process." That permits the Law of Allowance the scope to manifest what is invoked through the Law of Purposeful Intention (deliberate intention to create.) It is necessary to understand that in order for an intended creation to manifest, it must be *allowed* to manifest. This happens through holding the intention firmly in intellective view in the full faith and anticipation that it is already in energetic thought form and deliberately drawing to itself the molecular experiential format that will allow it to come into perceivable reality.

Embracing the Laws of the Universe as a viable method of bringing a new paradigm of experience to this planet and its inhabitants requires focusing committed intention through the understanding and application of the interacting sequence of the principles involved. These laws have been introduced in their most basic formats along with simple explanations of both the sequential and interacting processes that allow them to serve as a purposeful vehicle of creation. The Laws are responsive to intention and thus are often, if not most of the time, operating from a perspective of default, meaning they are manifesting whatever is being held in focus by any and all thought held in place. Thus those whose thoughts are on poverty and lack are creating within their experience more poverty and lack. Thoughts on victimhood are drawing more experiences of victimhood. Thoughts of hatred and revenge bring experiences of being hated and of vengeance. Focus on "wanting" particular experiences or things, brings more "wanting," not the manifestation of the objects of the wanting. Thoughts of appreciation of abundance, happiness and joy bring more of those. It all depends upon the perspective of the focusing conscious awareness.

The Laws are real and the results they bring forth when properly applied are real. The doubt that arises during the linear sequence of time that is experienced between the invocation of purposeful intent and the manifestation into realized experience is the trap. Manifestation between energetic thought formation of the matrix to the realizable experience varies with the quality of purposeful thought that is held in place during this interim. The quality is influenced greatly by the emotional excitement that is contained in the anticipation with which the event is awaited. Though emotional support is experienced periodically, it is difficult to maintain the necessary level of anticipation through "knowing" the matrix is indeed drawing to it the required condensing energy to bring about completion. Thus, it serves the process to have multiple foci contributing to the thought pool that is holding the pattern in place. Here again, it is the generally understood desire for a new paradigm of experience that is the organizing force fueled by the input of contributory data to support this desire from myriad points of view. The focused energy input within a delineated pattern that is defined within a process in harmony with the outflow of Universal expression moves through manifestation with a maximum of efficiency. By funneling the thought energies through an agreed upon organizing focus a dynamic is established that elicits an attractive force that brings to the process more thought energies that in turn adds further empowerment to all phases. Thus it is seen to build upon itself because it is acting in harmony with the creative outflow of potentiality which can be understood to be energy that is yet without purpose or form. This unformatted energy is more quickly imprinted with the desired expression. It is not necessary to break down or reformat energy already imprinted. Since the Law of Allowance is free to ascertain the most appropriate combination of available essential elements that will benefit the whole, manifestation is within a harmonious flow.

It is to be remembered that all manifestation that is attempted that is contrary to the creative flow that maintains the whole must of necessity by held tightly in focus within carefully delineated guidelines. All elements must be contained within the preset guidelines and error factors must be reviewed and corrections carefully made for any deviations. A monumental difference is experienced between the release of a freeflow of energy set into motion within universal harmonious guidelines and the focus required to direct those that deviate from that flow. The Laws working together freely have available self-direction within the process utilizing wisdom that is beyond comprehension. That is a decided advantage in the birthing of the new paradigm.

III-44

Each and all are surrounded by the energy that focuses the awareness that each knows as him or herself. It is the consciousness that allows choices and observation of the self within those choices. The variation and the extent that this selection involves varies with the willingness to confront the situations and circumstances that are present and to make decisions that encompass the range of greatest to the least effect upon the status quo each is experiencing. This begins during childhood. It is then that parents wield great influence through their approval or disapproval of the choices that each child makes. Until about the age of 12 parents are the "gods" of each child's life experience. The relationship established between the child and its parents influences the pattern of decision making that will be lived out during the rest of that lifetime. The child may decide to follow the pattern as set or they may choose to use it as a guide for change. Again, it is the conscious awareness making a decisive choice that will influence the pattern of the life experience. The confidence or lack of it that is acquired during childhood influences the courage and adventurousness that each applies during the life experience. They are further influenced not only by the input of other interactions and experiences but also by the genetic inclinations that are inherited through cellular memory passed on through previous experiences of prior generations. All of these influences are continuously interacting within the consciousness as well as those attachments that are made to objects, circumstances, situations and relationships with others. As the ability grows to interact with more and more influences in what is deemed the "modern world" with its global travel and global media exchanges, it is easily understood that life is anything but simple in this time and place.

It is considered progress to find the awareness surrounded by complexity. If that is true, then mankind should be extremely content and experiencing both mental and spiritual evolvement. A few are able to "put it all together," but certainly not a sufficient number to lift the conscious experience of the many. It then becomes necessary, if evolvement is to become a step forward, for a sufficient number to prioritize their life choices to bring this purpose into a meaningful focus. It has been the intent of these messages to assist in bringing the understanding of the necessity of doing just that in order that a shift in the planned future of mankind on this planet take place. It has been pointed out many times that it can only happen through the concerted efforts of enough individual humans by their own choice to do what is appropriate to cause this to happen. It must first begin within each individual self-awareness with the desire for it to happen on a planetary level. This is the foundation for all else to build upon. Each must understand that it is their rightful inheritance to take dominion over the direction of their evolvement. Until that choice of personal responsibility is made, some other unit of awareness will be happy to do it. The inheritance of the DNA used to introduce the original genetic enhancement that pushed the evolvement rapidly into self-awareness for those originally inhabiting this planet causes the natural group tendency to inevitably lead to competition and power struggles rather than cooperation. It therefore becomes clear that a purposeful choice must be made between competition and cooperation. This would lead to a major shift in the overall group experience. It would lead the human experience on a totally new path of expression. It seems such a simple choice in light of the profound change that would result. As is the case in all life experience, the simple choices are often the most profound and life changing.

While the messages are dealing with the simple truths that lie at the basis of evolving experience, the masters of control continue to complicate and confuse by causing chaos at points all over the planet. It is their plan to cause enough chaos and confusion to overwhelm their overly independent (in their opinion) workers into giving up any thoughts of freedom in order to have order and peace. As the confusion and chaos grow, all memories of the past seem to have had more of the order and peace that is desired. This is what is planned and presented through subtle suggestion. The more complex the experience surrounding humanity, the more easily it is believed it can be herded into asking for outside control to reorder their existence. Then it can be said, "humanity asked for their help!" It is in understanding their methodology that it can be clearly seen that in order to free itself, humanity must make exactly the opposite decision. It must decide that control by outsiders in the guise of "government," especially as "a single world government" will not bring about the desired Utopia. There must be a nucleus of informed and purposefully intending people that are committed to initiating an independent and free experience for this planet and its inhabitants. It must be clearly understand that this planet and its abundant resources rightfully belong to its human inhabitants to use for their own benefit to create an independent member of the galactic family. Help is available to initiate this opportunity. Advice to assist is available to be accepted or not, as chosen by those who take advantage of this opportunity.

These messages return again and again to the underlying theme of choice and responsibility. It is hoped that this understanding and this attitude are becoming a premise for the choices that are made by each individual. These individuals are now forming a growing nucleus of informed thought that is focused on the purposeful intent to claim the inheritance that belongs to the human population of this planet from this day forward in sequential timing. It can only be claimed by knowing it as truth and declaring it as the basis for every act of choice. Through purposefully desiring a new paradigm of experience, with cooperation as its focus of empowerment for "the highest and best good for all concerned," the energetic framework is put in place. The pattern then begins filling in as the harmony of agreement corresponds with the action of the Laws of the Universe. The ripples of added conscious agreement continues to build as the messages reach more and more people and the pattern strengthens. As the "ground crew" continues in their committed focus, so also does the anticipation that fuels the purposeful intent. Help in various forms of interventional formats begins to assist. These will not create the new paradigm, but will stand forth to allow the new pattern to formulate.

The term "ground crew" has never been meant to indicate that it is acting under the specific directions of outside help. It is meant to be understood that it is a cooperating group that is now receiving informational help to support them in completing the assignment that was agreed upon before incarnating in human bodies to assist in bringing this planet out of bondage and into the full opportunity to evolve. These have taken on the human limitations of their earthly genetic parent's histories, but have brought with them strengths to blend into the mix of evolutionary advancements made by those humans that have evolved or have been abandoned on this planet. These ask for nothing but the commitment and cooperative help of all who will understand the opportunity that is being offered. It matters not what the reason is that each individual volunteers. All are necessary contributors to a worthy and vastly rich opportunity at the individual and planetary level that will ripple outward to an extent that is beyond imagination. It is hoped that once the dream is birthed within each imagination it will take root and grow into an unshakable commitment that will fuel its purposeful focus through the chaos that is planned. This commitment will assist each to keep their equilibrium. Their example of courage and stability will in turn attract many to the cause of the liberation of humanity.

III-45

The understanding of time, space and reality present a great mystery to limited consciousness. The vibratory rate of manifested experience and observable matter or objects to be experienced in 3rd dimensional reality requires the concept of time to be comprehended within a sequential format. This requirement separates simultaneous events and manifestations into identifiable segments thus dividing multiple coactive happenings into recognizable units. It is then difficult to discern a reasonable and essentially accurate picture of complex situations using only the *known* pieces. Arriving at a bigger picture by assembling information from a stream of passing information requires a process necessitating the activation of a portion of the brain that is latent in most earthbound humans. The known factors may not contribute enough information to indicate the integral picture, but certainly the parts considered separately in no way indicate the combined elements forming what is true. In other words, the 3rd dimensional experience is extremely limiting. This is the reason it is so difficult to transcend it through individual effort. The addition of multiple media providing mass amounts of information has been instructive in allowing the realization that situations that are larger and more inclusive exist than are being revealed. The amount of conflicting and deliberately misleading data included in the available information makes accurate conclusions difficult to formulate. Situations change, the available information changes and the end result is overwhelm and confusion.

It is important to understand that the deliberate confusion that is being foisted upon humanity by the use of both ends of the information continuum is purposeful. Too much information along with too little truthful and pertinent information is presented simultaneously. This purposefully prohibits thoughtful and intelligent humans from deriving accurate conclusions and reasonably true pictures from the ongoing flow of information about events and situations. The frustrating search for needed information leads concerned members of humanity either to acquiesce or continue to search futilely in order to intuit at least an indication of the true scenario that is going on around them. Knowing there is no way to ascertain all the information, each draws conclusions in the best way possible and experiences confusion and distrust.

Is there a solution to this dilemma? Consider that it may be best to accept the situation as it appears. It is possible that the confusion and chaos that are planned for humanity to experience and accept are exactly the experience needed. It is expected that mankind will resist and condemn the chaotic conditions and desire an end. If instead these conditions are accepted as a part of the process of the eradication of the very chaos and confusion that are being experienced so that these can be replaced with a totally new experience, a shift in the total scenario is inevitable. Indeed, it can be considered that what is going on is inevitable. The current system must break down in order that a new one can be put in place. It provides the opportunity for mankind to intercede and create for itself what it desires.

The question at this time is what is it that mankind desires to create? It will be either a continuation of the colonization of this planet by outsiders or the declaration of sovereignty and ownership by asserting that the true ownership of this planet belongs to the evolving human population. To this end, these messages are dedicated to educating all humans who can be contacted, all those that will take up the gauntlet and recognize their true identity as citizens rather than owned slaves. These must dedicate their life focus to the purpose of declaring the freedom of the entire planet. The scope of thought must be toward recreating the whole. From this perspective it can be seen that the push for a global identity serves this purpose well. Indeed, there are no accidents. The impetus of the desire for the "highest and best good for all concerned" can and will use all facets of existing experience for the greater good when it is released and allowed to do so through focused and encompassing purposeful intent.

It requires mature and intelligent beings to thoughtfully consider an unprecedented plan of cooperation for a purpose of the highest possible intention for an entire civilization. This sets forth an opportunity that can, if considered, call forth the memory of the reason why each has incarnated at this time on this planet. All the experiences that have happened thus far in this lifetime pale when compared to the prospect of providing assistance to a beleaguered planet and its numerous inhabitants that are now denied their rightful freedom to evolve in a positive and supportive environment. This assistance would end the rape and pillage of a richly endowed planet and solar system that are now being used to support civilizations that have failed to care for their own planetary homes.

The change of consciousness from victim to sovereign responsibility is the necessary foundation for the fundamental change of the planetary experience. Commitment to a cooperative focus that clearly delineates the benefits available to be experienced is an impetus for joining a worthwhile cause. The individual as well as group benefits available for participation have been enumerated in past messages. The simple and yet incredibly effective factors to be contributed have also been listed. The opportunity to experience into wisdom through cooperating within the basic Laws of the Universe offers evolution possibilities that are rarely available in one lifetime. Seldom is such a "sales pitch" given to entice mesmerized units of consciousness to awaken and to activate their previously intended participation. However, this is a well orchestrated and long standing situation that is finally ripe for transition into a different manifestation of human experience. Full participation is welcome indeed.

III-46

The information as presented so far has brought forth for each individual a greater understanding of the reason each is present and what each has come forth to accomplish. There have been transitions to contemplate through considering possibilities of the origin and evolvement of mankind on this planet that are far different than those presented by mainstream religion and the organized scientific community. It is interesting to note that definite and thoroughly researched available artifacts found at many different sites around the planet support the theory of the forced evolution of the original life forms for the purpose of serving outside ownership interests. These facts logically fill in the gaps that the mainstream anthropologists are unable to explain and in doing so discredit their historical conjectures. Through the willingness to consider all the possibilities, including the two commonly debated conflicting origin theories, the thought process has been enhanced. Once "possibility thinking" has been incorporated into the mind/brain process, it changes the way all incoming information is considered. It is rather like breaking down a shell that has been artificially placed around each conscious awareness to protect it from considering anything other than the standard approved thought diet that is constantly fed to modern societies. This, of course, is purposeful to shape the collective/mass consciousness of the planetary whole to fit within the plan to control and re-engineer the human worker down the evolutionary scale rather than to allow it to spiral upward normally.

Once this understanding is firmly established in the minds of the readers of these messages, it naturally focuses the intent toward thwarting this plan by outsiders that is clearly only for their benefit. No intelligent conscious awareness desires devolution rather than evolution. It also becomes quite clear that in order to change the future experience, it is not possible to use methodology that has been purposefully introduced and encouraged by the outside influence that obviously has psychologically planned every human experience to fit within their overall strategy of control. It becomes necessary to understand that in order to outmaneuver these planners, it is necessary to move to a strategy that is at least one step above their model program procedures. Their methods of operation involve using the Universal Laws in a focus that is not in harmony with the flow of energy generated by the expression of pure potentiality into greater self-contemplation. The plan of devolution of the humans on this planet is in direct opposition to this flow. It is then obvious that the intent to create a different experience is established by purposefully invoking the Universal Laws to act within the flow that moves expansively through evolution of species.

There is no manifestation of experience or object without thought first conceiving and then projecting the desired design into the limitless field of undifferentiated energy that is available and waiting to fill the mold created by the intended design. When the Laws are invoked in harmony with their purpose and released to fill in the details of the basic pattern, wondrous results happen. In contrast, as has been stated previously, to use the Laws in a contrary flow, every detail must be delineated and held firmly in concentrated focus not only to create the design, but also to hold it in place. Consequently as the pattern becomes more and more detailed, it also becomes more and more fragile. If the focus is released, the natural "thought thinking" process would recognize the disharmony with its original purpose and begin a self-destruction process. The overview provided by this discussion allows for the reader to comprehend a larger picture/understanding of the situation in which the planet Earth and its inhabitants find themselves at this moment in its history. The word "transcend" means to "rise above, transform, excel." In order to continue on their path of evolution, humanity must "transcend" this current experience. To do that, it must "rise above" those that would thwart that natural progress. Because thought is the basis of creation, it then becomes apparent that mankind must "think" in a way that is "above and beyond" their jailers, using a "transformative" conceptual pattern as their basis of intent. This could be further assisted if variations appear in humanity's behavior pattern that is inconsistent with what is "expected" to be their reaction to the programmed plan of control. Variations in humanity's projected stereotype behavior cause attention to shift away from the concentration needed to hold their expanding pattern in place. This then would weaken their ability to hold their fragile model in form.

The question comes to mind as to how this all important "pattern of control" is held in place by the varied groups that make up the support focus provided by the members of humanity that are in league with those that are now in control of the planet. The answer is very simple! Ritual! At the basis of all-ritual, religious or fraternal, public or secret, either similar wording or similar intent is present. All of these are purposefully mind controlling and limit the behavior of those that take part in them even after these may have left the group and no longer practice the rituals. The concepts imparted continue to exert influence. The impact of participation in ritualistic routine designed to limit and control is thorough and often difficult to transcend. This is so because the patterns of limitation at the basis of its purpose tend to permeate many areas of thought and influence decisions that limit "possibility thinking." Are all rituals devolutional? That depends upon the basic purpose and whether or not those practicing the ritual remain free of any desire to control or use the ritual for any devious purpose. It is difficult to invoke and hold a ritual to its original intent for any length of use. Consequently, spontaneity in meditation/prayer is strongly suggested.

It may seem that just about all components of current life on the planet are tainted in some way with purposeful harm in mind. Certainly far-reaching efforts are being made to control every possible attitude and opinion. The human psyche has been examined extensively for the purpose of limiting and reversing the progress that has been made by the human beings either of origin or transplanted here. In actuality, because of the push to limit progress, the push to advance has been stronger than it would otherwise have been. It is difficult to limit further what has progressed despite great effort to prevent or lessen it. The only method employed by the self-appointed governors of the planet/solar system has been to do more of the same methods that have not stopped progress only slowed it down. It appears to be working with the large mass of individuals, however, as most of those reading these messages can testify, it took a brief encounter with a logical presentation of triggering ideas to introduce "possibility thinking" right through all the programming for limitation. That in itself should indicate the tenuous success of the plan that is being foisted on humanity. It is time to begin thinking independently including as many possibilities "as possible" about what is being provided as guidance from *all* sources meant to influence experiencing the gift of life. Consider the source and what might be the purposeful intent. Does it intend to promote opportunities to evolve or is it intended to limit, control and lead to the eventual lessening of possibilities to make purposeful independent choices for the highest and best good of all concerned? Intention is the measuring quality to carefully ascertain. However, the best intention based on (ritual) information designed to influence negatively, cannot but accomplish the original purpose or at the least, cause confusion. There are many opportunities for lessons in discernment. Observe and consider carefully rather than come to conclusions too quickly. If each one has clear and purposeful intent to be aligned with what is truly for the highest and best good for all concerned, the observation mode will provide a true sense of what are the appropriate determinations to be made.

III-47

The situation as it now exists as perceived reality is viewed by each individual through the screen of previous influences. These messages are literally sifted through the belief systems of each individual in a format that is acceptable to each as reality. As what is acceptable is incorporated within the current belief system, this then creates a new reality format. This is a constant and ongoing process with regard to all information received from all sources. How much change happens within each reality format depends upon the flexibility of the individual psyche. What is gleaned from the messages as acceptable information varies with each individual. What segments seem especially important to one individual will not necessarily seem important to another. This is the reason that each is encouraged to read and reread the information. As the reader accepts portions of the information as possibly true, the accepted reality format of that moment changes. Different perspectives of what is indicated through the wording are perceived and either accepted as possibilities or rejected with each reading. With repeated readings different information stands forth as especially meaningful and in turn stimulates new understandings as the mind/brain process is activated through consideration of different possibilities. It is a program designed to awaken and enhance the natural latent abilities yet to be tapped and to reawaken those that have been shut down by the mind control procedures all have been experiencing in increasing degrees for far longer than this century.

The process that is begun by reading and assimilating those facets of information that are accepted into the belief system causes a shift in the thought process that reaches into other areas of the life experience. While it is focused toward birthing a new paradigm of experience for the human experience on this planet, it brings with it other changes that will benefit those choosing to incorporate greater flexibility into their concept of experience within a body. Experiencing an active roll in the creation process at the present density of earth's vibratory level requires the ability to acknowledge, internalize, analyze, and express emotions within the purposeful intention of living within the "highest and best good of all concerned." This is setting up interaction that ripples outwardly in far reaching effects beyond the finite mind's ability to comprehend. It is the release of the format of experience that must limit to control that has its basis in fear. Control is believed to offset fear in order that change can be slowed and a modicum of "peaceful existence" can be experienced. However, the control mode requires more control measures to support the original limits and is a self-perpetuating negatively expanding cycle. It is the mode that has been adopted by those who would own and "control" this planet and its inhabitants. The intention to create within the Universal Laws focused for the "highest and best good for all concerned" deliberately invokes change. It is through the release of this intention into the Laws that change flows within a coordinated cycle that is logical and effortless. It is within this context that "freedom" is experienced. When all are included, then abundance is experienced in myriad different modes. Freedom encourages and allows diversity of expression whereas control demands conformity and limitation. Both of these are contrary to the natural desires of self-aware consciousness. This is because those that attained this higher state of awareness have done so by aligning themselves with the flow of greater self-contemplation that is at the basis of potentiality knowing itself through the expression of thought into experience into wisdom. It is through wisdom; knowledge acquired by living actual realized experience, that greater freedom is realized. This is the reason that life on a 3rd dimensional planet is honored and desired by units of self awareness. To "know" greatly accelerates the evolution of the greater soul matrix of which each is an intricate interactive part. Through this process, a greater understanding of who and what each one is becomes gradually acknowledged and realized. This carefully discovered self-realization is the foundation of all progress. Each recognition adds to the basic understanding, the knowing that each is an essential aspect of the essence of the whole. This whole is incomplete until the totality of it is gathered into the awareness of the true nature of whatever adventure is the focus to be thoroughly investigated and understood in this grand cycle.

Forever is incomprehensible. "Now" is the only segment of power available to the conscious awareness. 3rd dimensional awareness continues to focus on the past and the future, which removes the consciousness from participation in the only available point of influence. Past memory is meant to serve as an informational source to prevent repetition of previous inappropriate experience. The future is an unknowable point that is available to receive the experience that will manifest based on intentions and actions made in the "now" of the current moment. This unknown future cannot be different than what is being experienced in the current circumstances if there is no one present in the proactive moment acting in the creative intentional thought mode. It has been pointed out that if all the past and future thought was subtracted from the total human focused thought on this planet at any given second, there are very few people actually present. It is something to contemplate carefully.

The question then arises as to what is the difference between being absent in future thought and in intending a change to manifest in the future. When a conscious awareness is intending a creative thought, that awareness is experiencing as if it were actually present in the midst of the intended creation. In other words the future intention is being pulled into the present moment as if it already exists. The imagination has that individual either pictorially or emotionally or in both modes, experiencing what is intended as if it already exists in the present moment. How is that possible if only the basic framework is known? The answer is to pretend that it is known and play with what it might actually be like. Even if only one tiny segment of the whole is examined in the exercise of imagination and enough are simulating this, then a whole will formulate. The thought-thinking segment will coordinate and revise the complexities into a balanced and harmonious format that will exceed all expectations. The birth of the new paradigm of experience will begin the change by reorganizing mankind's daily happenings. Those that are the instruments of this change will desire big changes to happen quickly. However, small changes in many places and in many different occurrences will begin the shift. It is more difficult to plug many small holes in a wall of plans than a few large ones. Subtle energy at work in many places leads to profound change. Trust the process!

III-48

It is as though the planet itself is drawing a deep breath before it begins to literally shudder and shake in a effort to focus its energies toward saving itself from the abuse it is yet absorbing. In its collectivized thought process it seems to be coming to the conclusion that enough is enough and that it is time to begin a retaliating process in order to release itself from the relentless onslaught of destructive activities that its boarders are deliberately engaging in at "her" expense. As all manifestations are a balance of energies, it may be considered that the Earth is a "womb" or receiver/receptacle of the creative energies that are focused through the star (sun) energy that is the center of this planetary system. At the moment it is the only planet in this solar system supporting 3rd dimensional evolving humans on its surface.

While currently known history of this planet seems like a long time in the human reality system, planetary history covers what seems like measureless time periods when considered in a sequential time mode. Difficult as it is to encompass, there are other logical systems of perceiving the evolutionary process. When the brain/mind is fully activated, the ability to transcend the need to observe in a linear mode allows a shift to a process that relegates the resultant time factor from the controlling influence in observation to a variable of little importance. The process itself becomes the governing focus allowing the mind to become absorbed and to encompass the flow of multifaceted interaction within the "wholegraphic" scenario that is being played out. The ability to change the mode of observation through greater ability to observe the many parts of a whole interacting simultaneously changes the awareness of the self within this view of the unlimited movement of energies. As the perception expands to encompass the greater energetic picture, the self-awareness changes in correlation to this expansion of comprehension abilities. Through the expanded ability to perceive a situation from a more inclusive viewpoint, it is understood in a different dimensional point of view. In this way, it can be said that life is being experienced within a greater or higher dimensional plane of observation. This does not indicate an "easier" level of experience, but one that is more inclusive of causes and details that went unnoticed within prior available abilities. Acuity of thought along with the desire to know more in order to express more precede dimensional changes. In other words, the ability must be developed and practiced before it is possible to move into the higher dimensions of experience. The move does not come before the development of the skills to experience and maintain the necessary focus needed to remain at that dimensional level.

The shift to higher dimensions is earned (or remembered) by practicing now. At the basis of dimensional shifts is appreciation of the gift of self-awareness. This is not accomplished through or in tandem with self-deprecation. The "self" always does the best it can within the environment that is provided by its own surrounding thoughts. As it is immersed in self-appreciation it grows in expression. However, if surrounded by criticism and thoughts that belittle it, it shrinks and is robbed of the ability to express its Life energy effectively. The difference between self-appreciation and self-aggrandizement must be thoroughly understood. The important factor is whether or not the process is based on comparison to/with others. What is considered within the self without the necessity of measuring/comparing the self to others is the key. Each rises within its own world of self-awareness. What others think or what self thinks it has accomplished compared to others is of no value in the overall journey through 3rd dimensional experience. Each journey is self-contained.

Others are present as mirrors in which to observe the self. What is seen in others is the reflection of what the self is unable to see by looking within. It is said that, "each is alone in a hall of mirrors." Until the self is willing to recognize "itself" in these mirrors, there is no way to find the door out of the hall. Finding the door already open is always a surprise, for it is impossible to determine when one has reached the ability to embody the facets of self-awareness necessary to integrate into the next dimensional experience. Much hype is circulating about the shift in the earth's vibrations that will "carry" its inhabitants to a higher dimension. It is firmly stated here and now that humanity's capability to exist at the next higher level of dimensional experience will determine whether or not individuals will make that change. The earth can and will make such a shift. How many will accompany her in that shift will be determined by those individuals themselves based on their personal abilities earned through appreciation of the "personal self" and their ability to allow an expansion of their thought processes into new possibilities of experiencing what surrounds them here and now.

The ability to release old familiar comfort zones and *allow* participation in creating a new paradigm of experience is far more challenging than is imagined when it is first considered. Adventure sounds intriguing; however, stepping off the cliff into unknowable new experiences without any familiar frame of reference requires commitment and a large measure of courage. If it were not for the horror of "knowing" the truth of the genocide and enslavement that is planned; few would have the necessary incentive or courage to make the choice. It is simply an "either-or" choice. There is no in-between place to go. Looking at it from that perspective, certainly creating a new experience based on self appreciation that transcends the victim experience is far more appealing than riding the descending spiral into a long standing greater victimhood. There are no rescuers in sight that care to become involved with those with too few "guts" to help themselves. The opportunity to continue this current experience of learning how to pull the self up by its own bootstraps through self-appreciation and possibility thinking is waiting elsewhere for the stubborn and the fainthearted. The choice to be part of this scenario on this planet at this time is not/was not an accident. You are here by choice to make a further choice. It is suggested that you do it and do it with style and enthusiasm!

III-49

The copies of the *Handbook for the New Paradigm* now circulating can be counted in the thousands, and *Embracing the Rainbow* in the hundreds. Each one is causing a ripple of change in the consciousness of the reader and in turn within the mass consciousness. The books are now traveling to many countries so that the change can begin to be worldwide. It is hoped that translations will be made and copies of these circulated. It is necessary that the focus of cooperation in creating a different experience become a global influence. Countries where the population has little or no access to communications other than government propaganda will require intervention of another kind. Trust that this problem is being given very special attention. Also, remember the hundredth monkey theory. In this case, include a request for special methods of reaching these fellow humans in prayer and meditations. Help can be given for the highest and best good of those segments of humanity when it is requested for them. In reality it is in support of what they are already asking for themselves. The tighter the oppressive situation, the greater the silent outcry of those experiencing it. Freedom to evolve is innately desired by all from the deepest levels of awareness. What may not be spoken, can be thought with great emotion.

Though emphasized frequently throughout the messages, the power of thought as the prerequisite for the spoken word is powerful indeed. When thoughts and words are focused by many in agreement with passion and enthusiasm, a momentum is built to manifest the desired intention. As more contribute added momentum, the ripples become waves. When agreement and cooperation focus a positive desire for the highest and best good possible, there is little that can prevent the manifestation of what is intended. What is crucial to understand is that in the process of the creation of the new, the old must cease to exist, for both cannot share the same space, except as one is declining and the new is coming into reality. As this process is being experienced, it is critical that the focus be held firmly in place because it would be easy to interpret the necessary period of chaos and confusion as failure rather than to see it as *the beginning stages of success.* It is extremely important that all members of the "ground crew" have a firm understanding of the purpose of the period of chaos. It must happen in order to clear away the old and make space for the new. It also provides added available energies to be siphoned from the chaos and reformatted into the new intended pattern.

It will be very challenging to acknowledge the breaking down of personal life patterns when they happen to each one as well as many others and know it is absolutely necessary in order to manifest a vastly improved way of life. This is the reason that the messages began with admonitions to prepare for change in the best ways possible. This is extremely challenging in view of the urban life style the majority of "modern" humanity lives, depending on the availability of food from stores and restaurants that require supplies to be delivered daily from far away sources. Jobs depend on utilities and lines of communications, for few produce actual products that would aid in survival. 50 years ago, in times of stress, most people had family living on farms that could assist in providing basic food necessities for at least a period of time. Even in what is called 3rd world countries, the small farmers have been pushed off their land to make way for "factory farming operations." Humanity has allowed itself to be placed in dire straits indeed for basic survival needs are controlled and in short supply worldwide. This information is not for the purpose of promoting fear, but so that each may consider carefully what is not only possible, but also probable in the near future. Those that have given little concern for the plight of the farmer/rancher in the past should now understand and rethink their concerns. The push is on to eliminate those that have survived. These are a tenacious and efficient group that have constantly devised ways to stay on the land. There are too few of them left to feed the urban multitudes outside the established import system. This is a true picture worldwide.

Humans, when there is necessity, can be amazingly creative. But could the modern urban dweller survive if all the modern conveniences were to disappear? Those who have spent their lives in an urban environment would do well to research and plan some "what if" scenarios with their families. What would be true necessities if there were only crickets for entertainment? Basic survival necessities are seldom found in the modern urban household. If the faucets don't provide water, where would it be found and how could it be made drinkable? It is time to consider this basic issue with logic and planning. The answers will not be found on TV, in videos or the movies. There are excellent "homesteading" information sources available—magazines and books. There are military survival handbooks, etc. Some are out of print and difficult, but not impossible to find. It would be wise to consider priorities and perhaps consider different choices with regard to what can be acquired and stored to satisfy possible future requirements.

III-50

The greatest understanding that enables the limited mind to connect with the totality of Universal existence is through mathematics. Energy exists within precise cycles that can be read as mathematical equations. In order for Universal existence to continue, all the pieces of the puzzle must fit together. Since life expressing is not a static existence, that indicates that changes are going on within the totality of the puzzle on a continuing basis. Variations are constantly being recalculated to continue their inclusion within the whole, which is far greater than can be imagined by finite minds. Thus it is that catastrophic events cause chaos and recalculation down to intricate details and these ripple outward influencing the Universal whole. The greater the catastrophe, the greater the chaos during the period of restoring unanimity. Knowing this, great focus is concentrated on areas to prevent such happenings if possible, or at least to lessen the causative factors. This is not always possible for the "free will" factor of those intent on causing such episodes cannot be denied. If all the individuals within the area of disharmony are not in agreement with the disruptive focus, then there can be intervening action to counterbalance the intended disruptive action if those in disagreement specifically ask for help to offset the intended plans. Agreement with the disruptive plans does not need to be informed agreement. In other words, the plans need not be generally known or understood. Passive agreement through ignorance is still agreement.

This is the reason that so much effort has been put forth by various individuals and organizations to alert and inform the people of this planet that there is indeed a subversive plan moving toward completion. This plan, if allowed to reach completion, will deny natural evolvement of life on this planet and will allow survival and enslavement of only chosen ideal candidates. Those who do become aware of and choose not to agree with these plans must then come together in agreement to focus on a plan of their own to create a different scenario for the populace and ask for what is called Divine intervention. However, this cannot be asked of an unknowable God that may capriciously choose whether to answer or not, depending on His mood that day. Such a God does not exist. Pure potentiality exists with multiple levels of awareness within its expression all the way "down" to 3rd dimensional awareness and even below that level. All these multiple levels of awareness combined may indeed be considered "God." There are levels within this composite of awareness that are very great indeed. Consequently certain levels of this "God Awareness" can and do hear and answer prayers that are addressed to them correctly, either accidentally or through the understanding and application of the Basic Laws that all manifested awareness exists within.

To ask is the first important step. To continue to ask never allows the process to move beyond the asking stage. First ask, *assume* the answer is on its way and then continue to *express appreciation* that it is happening in its own perfect wisdom and timing. That "wisdom and timing" is greatly influenced by the one asking and how well that awareness is able to follow through with the two remaining steps after the initial asking. This is often called prayer. Nothing can happen until there is first asking. Then the next two steps, assuming it is happening (continued focus of intent) and expression of appreciation (allowance) controls the manifestation. It is that simple! A few additional details are helpful. Ask within a framework that allows what might be called "Divine Intelligence" or thought thinking to fill in the details. Doubt destroys results; trust insures them. It seems that these simple rules cannot be repeated too often, for habits formed through misinformation are difficult to overcome. It would be wise to reread this message frequently to remember these essential steps.

"Divine Intelligence" encompasses the benevolent galactic brothers, sisters and androgynous beings that have evolved beyond your level. It is true that there are those who live in harmony within the "God Energies" that promote evolvement at all levels of potentiality expressing itself. This is the composite of all accumulated wisdom knowing itself and continuing its expansive experience. All awareness is a part of that magnificent pool of intelligence. It is also true that through free will, there are those that are experiencing in disharmony with expansive intent. It is important to understand that self-awareness can purposefully destroy itself by continuing its negative experience to the point of destruction, because the negative focus lessens (literally pinches off) the focusing energies of the soul. However destruction by this method of weakening the connection to the soul is very difficult to do. Awareness can "muck around" in negative experiences for the learning that can be gained and then return to harmonious experience.

Many of those that might be considered to have great wisdom and experience have pursued both paths. To have a body destroyed by those experiencing within what is considered negative experience does not destroy the self-awareness. In other words, unless deliberately chosen, there is no real death, just the need to digest the learning available from the victim experience, then acquire a new body to continue the next experiencing opportunity into wisdom and evolve within the field of potentiality. The availability of bodies is sometimes limited and thus it is suggested to use the present one to the greatest advantage possible while you have it. Honor it and care for it. It is intended that a radiant "being" express love and caring for all "life" through it by thoughts, words and deeds. Align the overall individual intention with that framework and positive results happen.

III-51

Though often a topic of discussion, the number of humans that this planet can provide for comfortably within its ecosystem is not the real determining factor in the overall "health" of the planet. The deciding capability is determined by how the resources are shared and for what intent these are used by the inhabitants. If the intent is for the "highest and best good" of *all* the inhabitants and these are shared in ways that provide for an abundant life experience for all, then the carrying capacity of inhabitants on the planet is considerably greater. It is obvious that that does not describe the current situation. It is also patently obvious that the current situation cannot continue if the planet is to sustain itself in its present form. The current story line can only end in disaster for both the inhabitants and the planet itself. Observation of the other planets in the solar system with no apparent life on their surfaces is the stark reality and a possible end to the continuation of the push for luxury for the privileged at the expense of the remainder of humanity and the planet's natural environment.

The ability of the planet itself to absorb the escalating misuse of its resources while the majority of its inhabitants are in suffering and misery is causing a shift in the energy that constitutes what can be called its "harmony quotient." In other words, the totality of the planetary awareness, which it definitely does possess, is becoming unstable or troubled. It too is aware that a progressive disharmony is being experienced in an increasing momentum that is continuously stimulated by deliberate intent. It might be said that the alarm bell has been ringing within that awareness for some time now causing the planet to now know that it is time to begin survival maneuvers or its current mode of expression will end. Because of the awesome power of the weaponry of both the planetary inhabitants and those vying to "own" this planet, its total destruction is not outside the realm of possibility. This precarious plight is now known to the totality of awareness that governs the action/reaction of the planetary processes that are what is called "nature." The sum total of mining, tremendous weights of water held within dams, surface and underground construction and weapons testing has caused internal pressure anomalies within the planet that are causing the various natural fracture lines to become extremely unstable. These fracture lines remain from previous pressure anomalies and as natural "zippers" to allow for normal shifts and changes in surface features. Add to this the contents of the mass consciousness that include pain, starvation, disease and an enormous outcry for change and relief. This exists along with the opposite intent to compress the human awareness into a weaker and weaker embodiment. The planetary awareness takes all these factors into account and must find a way to relieve all this pressure in the only way it can, which is what is currently termed "earth changes." These amount to changes in weather, volcanic eruptions and earthquakes. Each are in truth messages from the planet asking for the stress to be reduced by removing the causes of the stress. Unless this happens, these messages will become more and more urgent, that is more and more powerful. Unfortunately, many of the humans present within areas receiving the messages are caught up in the phenomena and the aftermath of the messages. The planetary choices are made in the areas where the greatest weakness is found in the earth's surface areas. Often phenomena return to the same areas because these still contain the weakest points. A shift of great enough proportion has not taken place for there to be a weaker point elsewhere on the planetary surface. Other factors enter into the greater picture. The focus of consciousness with regard to concern for the planet and its inhabitants helps to balance that area and relieve the planetary stress. It is a form of protection for that area. In this way, often the timetable of factual predictions of future happenings is slowed or prevented. The mass consciousness of humanity is a powerful component of the planetary whole. That is the reason that such an intense effort has been made to instill involuntary endorsement of the plan for continued outside ownership by the majority of human inhabitants. Deliberate misinformation and mind control from multiple sources have controlled the basis of human experience for generations in preparation for the favorable shift in multiple cosmic cycles that is happening now and in the near future. With the unsuspecting consent of a large segment of the mass consciousness, it can be said that Earth's citizens do not want a change and are cooperating with the outside influences. This is an effort to prevent "Divine intervention." Humanity on the one hand is asking for help and an end to the wars designed to keep them quarreling among themselves and unaware of the influence being exerted on their thought processes. The human race is being divided so that it can be conquered with the least effort.

It is appropriate to note here again that there is just "one human race" regardless of its diversity of appearance. All experience the "life force" identically. Only the outside appearances are different. These differences have been exploited along with cultural and religious variations to promote separation. All bodily, cultural and religious differences are responsibilities to learn of human unity within diversity. There is no advancement to higher dimensions until that truth is experienced into wisdom. Each has experienced within the different cultures to experience this reality into wisdom. It is important to the goals of the controllers that you forget those experiences and focus on the differences rather than the similarities. The similarities far outnumber the differences! It is to be noted that many of those experiencing in the higher dimensional realms are far different in appearance than those the human race sees within itself. Your "space" movies are quite accurate in imagining possible variations of species. Think about how that might be dealt with in the future, if it is possible to come together as a single human race, celebrate and maintain the diversity within it and create a new experience.

Epilogue

Those that read and study these three instructional manuals now view the current life experience on planet Earth from an entirely new point of view. This point of view is one that shifts daily as new information is absorbed, considered and incorporated into the belief system. As a foundation is built from which to view the experiences of life, it is constantly shifting. What seemed absolutely true in the recent past, often must be discarded for the wholistic picture changes to incorporate new information and revisions made by the choices of those that share the planetary whole. Through this understanding it becomes obvious that rigid and dogmatic doctrines obstruct the evolutionary progress of those that choose to allow themselves to become trapped in those belief structures. This constantly changing flow of opportunities to choose presents lessons in discernment with respect to the truth and applicability of new information. Each must consider how the new information might alter their perspective and decide if incorporating this change will allow the new view point to represent what is believable truth. In other words, it is necessary to "try the new information on for size" and then decide whether or not to accept it. While logic is an important testing tool, it is how the new picture *feels* that determines whether it is accepted or not.

When first encountering the new concepts that may be included in these messages, many will have put the book(s) aside for a period of time. These will return to reread and study them, for the daily situations that are observed from a new viewpoint will cause the truth of the messages to become clear. Some will reject them entirely, but will pass the book on to others that will resonate with the truth of them. In this way these will have fulfilled their contribution to creating the new paradigm of experience. As each reacts appropriately to this information, the purposeful intention to create a new experience for the planet and its inhabitants comes more clearly into manifestation. Already the energies are gathering as the concentration of intention attracts more participants. Responsive enthusiasm grows as it is realized that it is possible to transcend the current circumstances and create an entirely new situation that humanity has longed to experience by utilizing the Universal Laws that govern the progression of life's natural process.

Whether humanity remains stuck within its current reality or chooses to lift itself out by its own volition remains to be determined. Only through discarding the "poor us" syndrome and realizing that the power to bring about change lies within their own attitude and choices will the circumstances be reconstructed positively. Mankind must grow itself into true Hu-mans (god-men/women). Natural evolutionary progress, despite all attempts to prevent it, has made this potentiality for this change available now. It is hoped mankind will take full advantage of this significant opportunity.

Handbook for the New Paradigm

The messages contained in this handbook are intended to lift mankind from the entrapment of the victim consciousness that keeps the level of experience ensnared in fear and frustration. Humanity was intended to live, not in luxury, but in abundance. The information found between its covers will lead all that read and reread with an open mind to the discovery of the truth of who and what they truly are. The end of the search for these answers is provided at last in clarity and conciseness.

There are no recriminations or feelings of guilt to be gleaned from these pages. There is clarity and upliftment in each segment. It is the intent and purpose of this small book to encourage every reader to live in accordance with the plainly disclosed simple laws that underlay *all* that each comprehends as life. Each segment leads to greater understanding and to a simple application that encompasses them in entirety in a few words that guarantee absolute change in your day to day experience. You have only to think or speak them with diligence and sincerity at every appropriate opportunity. To become is your purpose and your heritage.

Embracing the Rainbow

This book, "Embracing the Rainbow, Volume II of the Handbook For The New Paradigm" contains the next series of messages guiding its readers to accept the concepts contained within them for the purpose of creating a new life experience for the "humans becoming" on planet Earth. Each message broadens the conceptual understandings of the necessity to release the limitations that have been thrust upon humanity preventing them from understanding who and what they truly are. It contains surprising truths of some of the shocking deceptions intentionally taught that limit and separate mankind from their opportunities for spiritual evolvement. It defines how it is possible to take back the heritage of self-determination, freely create ones own destiny and heal the planet and humanity as a whole living entity through the suggested dynamic process.